Congressional
Research
Service

Child Support Enforcement Program Incentive Payments: Background and Policy Issues

Carmen Solomon-Fears
Specialist in Social Policy

May 2, 2013

Congressional Research Service

7-5700

www.crs.gov

RL34203

CRS Report for Congress ———————————————————

Prepared for Members and Committees of Congress

Summary

The Child Support Enforcement (CSE) program, enacted in 1975, to help strengthen families by securing financial support from noncustodial parents, is funded with both state and federal dollars. The federal government bears the majority of CSE program expenditures and provides incentive payments to the states (which include Washington, DC, and the territories of Guam, Puerto Rico, and the Virgin Islands) for success in meeting CSE program goals. In FY2011, total CSE program expenditures amounted to $5.7 billion. The aggregate incentive payment amount to states was $513 million in FY2011.

P.L. 105-200, the Child Support Performance and Incentive Act of 1998, established a revised incentive payment system that provides incentive payments to states based on a percentage of the state's CSE collections and incorporates five performance measures related to establishment of paternity and child support orders, collections of current and past-due support payments, and cost-effectiveness. P.L. 105-200 set specific annual caps on total federal incentive payments and required states to reinvest incentive payments back into the CSE program. The exact amount of a state's incentive payment depends on its level of performance (or the rate of improvement over the previous year) when compared with other states. In addition, states are required to meet data quality standards. If states do not meet specified performance measures and data quality standards, they face federal financial penalties.

P.L. 109-171 (the Deficit Reduction Act of 2005) prohibited federal matching (effective October 1, 2007, i.e., FY2008) of state expenditure of federal CSE incentive payments. However, in 2009 P.L. 111-5 (the American Recovery and Reinvestment Act of 2009) required the Department of Health and Human Services (HHS) to temporarily provide federal matching funds (in FY2009 and FY2010) on CSE incentive payments that states reinvested back into the CSE program. Thus (since FY2011), CSE incentive payments that are received by states and reinvested in the CSE program are no longer eligible for federal reimbursement. The FY2008 repeal of federal reimbursement for incentive payments reinvested in the CSE program garnered much concern over its fiscal impact on the states and renewed interest in the incentive payment system per se.

A comparison of FY2002 incentive payment performance score data to FY2011 performance score data shows that CSE program performance has improved with respect to all five performance measures. Although CSE incentive payments were awarded to all 54 jurisdictions in FY2002, FY2005, FY2010, and FY2011 (the years covered in this report), some jurisdictions performed poorly on one or more of the five performance measures. Even so, on the basis of the unaudited FY2011 performance incentive scores of the 54 jurisdictions, 53 jurisdictions received an incentive for all five performance measures, and 1 jurisdiction (the Virgin Islands) received an incentive for four performance measures.

Despite a general consensus that the CSE program is doing well, questions still arise about whether the program is effectively meeting its mission and concerns exist over whether the program will be able to meet future expectations. Several factors may cause a state not to receive an incentive payment that is commensurate with its relative performance on individual measures. These factors include static or declining CSE collections; sliding scale performance scores that financially benefit states at the upper end (but not the top) of the artificial threshold and financially disadvantaged states at the lower end of the artificial threshold; a limited number of performance indicators that do not encompass all of the components critical to a successful CSE program; and a statutory maximum on the aggregate amount of incentive payments that can be paid to states. These factors are discussed in the context of the following policy questions: (1) Does the CSE incentive payment system reward good performance? (2) Should incentive payments be based on additional performance indicators? (3) Should Temporary Assistance for Needy Families (TANF) funds be reduced because of poor CSE performance? (4) Why aren't the incentives and penalties consistent for the paternity establishment performance measure? (5) Should incentive payments be based on individual state performance rather than aggregate state performance? and (6) Will the elimination of the federal match of incentive payments adversely affect CSE programs?

Contents

Figures

Tables

Appendixes

Contacts

Introduction

Since the Child Support Enforcement (CSE) program's enactment in 1975, the federal government has paid incentives (monetary payments) to states to encourage them to operate efficient and effective CSE programs.[1] The incentive payment system is part of the CSE program's strategic plan that rewards states for working to achieve the goals and objectives of the program. Incentive payments, although small when compared to federal reimbursement payments for state and local CSE activities, are a very important component of the CSE financing structure. Together with the incentive payment system is a penalty system that imposes financial penalties on states that fail to meet certain performance levels. The purpose of the two complementary systems is to reward states for results while holding them accountable for poor performance, thereby motivating states to focus their efforts on providing vital CSE services.

Before FY2008, the federal government was required to match incentive funds that states reinvested in the CSE program, at a federal matching rate of 66%. P.L. 109-171 (the Deficit Reduction Act of 2005) prohibits federal matching (effective October 1, 2007) of state expenditure of federal CSE incentive payments.[2] This means that CSE incentive payments that are received by states and reinvested in the CSE program are no longer eligible for federal reimbursement. The repeal of federal matching funds for incentive payments reinvested in the CSE program garnered much concern over its fiscal impact on the states and renewed interest in the incentive payment system per se. Given the loss of that funding source and the resulting cost shift to the states (during a time when many interests are competing for limited state dollars), attention has focused on the individual elements of the performance-based incentive payment system and whether they need to be modified to ensure that the CSE program remains effective and efficient.

This report describes the current CSE incentive payment system, provides information on financial penalties that are imposed on states if incentive payment data are unreliable or if performance standards are not met, explains how state incentive payments are derived, discusses some of the state trends, and presents some policy issues concerning incentive payments.

In addition, the report includes two appendices. **Appendix A** presents a legislative history of CSE incentive payments. **Appendix B** includes several detailed state tables that display unaudited incentive performance scores for each of the five performance measures.[3] **Table B-1** shows the amount of incentive payments received by states for FY2002, FY2005, FY2010, and FY2011. **Table B-2** displays unaudited incentive performance scores for each of the five performance measures for FY2002. **Table B-3** displays unaudited incentive performance scores for each of the five performance measures for FY2005. **Table B-4** displays unaudited incentive performance scores for each of the five performance measures for FY2010.

---

[1] The 1975 enacting legislation (P.L. 93-647) based incentive payments solely on child support collections made on behalf of welfare (i.e., Aid to Families with Dependent Children (AFDC)) families. In 1984, pursuant to P.L. 98-378, the law expanded the incentive payments formula to include child support collections made on behalf of nonwelfare families. For a legislative history of CSE incentive payments, see **Appendix A**. Also note that the AFDC entitlement program was replaced by the Temporary Assistance for Needy Families (TANF) block grant pursuant to P.L. 104-193 (the 1996 welfare reform law).

[2] P.L. 109-171, effective October 1, 2007, prohibited federal matching of state expenditure of federal CSE incentive payments. However, P.L. 111-5 required HHS to temporarily provide federal matching funds (in FY2009 and FY2010) on CSE incentive payments that states reinvest back into the CSE program. Thus, starting again in FY2011, CSE incentive payments that are received by states and reinvested in the CSE program are no longer eligible for federal reimbursement.

[3] The unaudited incentive performance scores are readily available each year when the federal Office of Child Support Enforcement (OCSE) publishes its preliminary data report. In this report the unaudited scores serve as a proxy for the actual (audited) performance indicator scores upon which actual incentive payments are based. (OCSE does not consistently publish actual (audited) performance indicator scores.)

Table B-5 displays unaudited incentive performance scores for each of the five performance measures for FY2011.

Background

The CSE program was enacted in 1975 as a federal-state-local partnership. It helps strengthen families by securing financial support from noncustodial parents. The CSE program serves both welfare and non-welfare families. In FY2011, the CSE program collected $27.3 billion in child support payments and served 15.8 million child support cases. In FY2011, total CSE program expenditures amounted to $5.7 billion, of which $513 million were incentive payments (i.e., 9% of total program expenditures). In FY2011, the CSE program collected $5.12 in child support (from noncustodial parents) for every dollar spent on the program. The CSE program is funded with both state and federal dollars. The federal government bears the majority of CSE program expenditures and provides incentive payments to the states for success in meeting CSE program goals.[4]

Financing Elements of the CSE Program

There are five funding streams for the CSE program. (For more details, see CRS Report RL33422, *Analysis of Federal-State Financing of the Child Support Enforcement Program*, by Carmen Solomon-Fears.)

First, states spend their own money to operate a CSE program; the level of funding allocated by the state and localities determines the amount of total resources available to CSE agencies.

Second, the federal government reimburses each state 66% of all allowable expenditures on CSE activities. The federal government's funding is "open-ended" in that it pays its percentage of expenditures by matching the amounts spent by state and local governments with no upper limit or ceiling. The federal government's financial participation in the CSE program is the program's largest revenue source.

Third, the federal government provides states with an incentive payment to encourage them to operate effective programs.[5] Federal law requires states to reinvest CSE incentive payments back into the CSE program or related activities. Effective October 1, 2007, P.L. 109-171 (enacted February 8, 2006) prohibited federal matching of state expenditures of federal CSE incentive payments. However, in 2009 P.L. 111-5 required HHS to temporarily provide federal matching funds (in FY2009 and FY2010) on CSE incentive payments that states reinvest back into the CSE program. Thus, starting again in FY2011, CSE incentive payments that are received by states and reinvested in the CSE program are no longer eligible for federal reimbursement.

Fourth, states collect child support on behalf of families receiving Temporary Assistance for Needy Families (TANF) to reimburse themselves (and the federal government) for the cost of TANF cash payments to the family. Federal law requires families who receive TANF cash assistance to assign their child support rights to the state in order to receive TANF. In addition, such families must cooperate with

---

[4] For additional information on the CSE program, see CRS Report RS22380, *Child Support Enforcement: Program Basics*, by Carmen Solomon-Fears.

[5] A 2011 report found that in aggregate about 16% of the state's share of CSE expenditures is financed with incentive payments. Source: Child Support Enforcement: Departures from Long-term Trends in Sources of Collections and Caseloads Reflect Recent Economic Conditions, U.S. Government Accountability Office, GAO-11-196, January 2011, p. 6.

the state if necessary to establish paternity and secure child support. CSE collections on behalf of families receiving TANF cash benefits are used to reimburse state and federal governments for TANF payments made to the family (i.e., child support payments go to the state instead of the family, except for amounts that states choose to "pass through" to the family as additional income that does not affect TANF eligibility or benefit amounts).

The formula for distributing the child support payments collected by the states on behalf of TANF families between the state and the federal government is still based on the old Aid to Families with Dependent Children (AFDC) federal-state reimbursement rates,[6] even though the AFDC entitlement program was replaced by the TANF block grant program.[7] Under existing law, states have the option of giving some, all, or none of their share of child support payments collected on behalf of TANF families to the family. Pursuant to P.L. 109-171 (effective October 1, 2008), states that choose to pass through some of the collected child support to the TANF family do not have to pay the federal government their shares of such collections if the amount passed through to the family and disregarded by the state does not exceed $100 per month ($200 per month for a family with two or more children) in child support collected on behalf of a TANF (or foster care) family. (For additional information, see CRS Report RL34105, *The Financial Impact of Child Support on TANF Families: Simulation for Selected States*, by Carmen Solomon-Fears and Gene Falk.)

Fifth, application fees and costs recovered from nonwelfare families help finance the CSE program. In the case of nonwelfare families, the custodial parent can hire a private attorney or apply for CSE services on their own. The CSE agency must charge an application fee, not to exceed $25, for families not on welfare who apply for CSE services. The CSE agency may charge this fee to the applicant or the noncustodial parent, or pay the fee out of state funds. In addition, a state may at its option recover costs in excess of the application fee. Such recovery may be either from the custodial parent or the noncustodial parent. Fees and costs recovered from nonwelfare cases must be subtracted from the state's total administrative costs before calculating the federal reimbursement amount (i.e., the 66% matching rate).

Moreover, effective October 1, 2006, P.L. 109-171 requires families that have never been on TANF to pay a $25 annual user fee when child support enforcement efforts on their behalf are successful (i.e., at least $500 annually is collected on their behalf). The state can collect the user fee from the custodial parent, the noncustodial parent, or the state can pay the fee out of state funds. This annual user fee is separate from the application fee.[8]

---

[6] Under old AFDC law, the rate at which states were reimbursed by the federal government for the costs of cash welfare was the Federal Medical Assistance Percentage (FMAP), which varies inversely with state per capita income (i.e., poor states have a higher federal matching rate, wealthy states have a lower federal matching rate). The FMAP ranges from a minimum of 50% to a statutory maximum of 83%. Like the old AFDC program, current law requires that child support collections made on behalf of welfare (i.e., TANF) families be split between the federal and state governments according to the FMAP. If a state has a 50% FMAP, the federal government is reimbursed $50 for each $100 in child support collections for TANF families; if a state has a 70% FMAP, the federal government is reimbursed $70 for each $100 in child support collections for TANF families. In the first example, the state keeps $50 and in the second example, the state keeps $30. Thus, states with a larger FMAP keep a smaller portion of the child support collections.

[7] The TANF block grant replaced the AFDC entitlement program pursuant to P.L. 104-193, the 1996 welfare reform law. Because the CSE incentive payments have changed significantly since 1975 (when the CSE program was enacted), this report refers to both AFDC families/cases and TANF families/cases, depending on the time frame.

[8] See CRS Report RS22753, *Child Support Enforcement: $25 Annual User Fee*, by Carmen Solomon-Fears.

Cap on Incentive Payments

As mentioned earlier, from the outset incentive payments were provided by the federal government to the states to encourage them to operate effective CSE programs. The 1996 welfare reform law (P.L. 104-193) required the Secretary of the Department of Health and Human Services (HHS), in consultation with state CSE directors, to develop and recommend to Congress a new incentive payment system that was revenue neutral. A report on CSE Incentive Funding was presented to Congress in February 1997.

P.L. 105-200, the Child Support Performance and Incentive Act of 1998 (enacted July 16, 1998), replaced the old incentive payment system to states[9] with a revised revenue-neutral (with respect to the federal government) incentive payment system that (1) provided incentive payments based on a percentage of the state's CSE collections; (2) incorporated five performance measures related to establishment of paternity and child support orders, collections of current and past-due child support payments, and cost-effectiveness; (3) phased in the incentive system, with it being fully effective beginning in FY2002; (4) required reinvestment of incentive payments into the CSE program; and (5) used an incentive payment formula weighted in favor of TANF and former TANF families.[10]

The requirement that the new incentive payment system be revenue neutral resulted in an annual cap on incentive payments. Congress capped incentive payments by legislating the total amount of incentive payments that states (in aggregate) could earn in each fiscal year. Federal law stipulated that the aggregate incentive payment to the states could not exceed the following amounts: $422 million for FY2000, $429 million for FY2001, $450 million for FY2002, $461 million for FY2003, $454 million for FY2004, $446 million for FY2005, $458 million for FY2006, $471 million for FY2007, and $483 million for FY2008. Since FY2008, the aggregate incentive payment to the states has been increased to account for inflation.[11] Congress based the capped aggregate incentive payment amount on Congressional Budget Office (CBO) projections of incentive payments at the time that the Child Support Performance and Incentive bill was passed.[12]

Purpose of the Current CSE Incentive Payment System

P.L. 105-200, the Child Support Performance and Incentive Act of 1998, revised the original incentive payment system in an effort to further improve the CSE program by linking incentive payments to states'

---

[9] Under the old incentive payment system, each state received a minimum incentive payment equal to at least 6% of the state's total amount of child support collections made on behalf of AFDC/TANF families for the year, plus at least 6% of the state's total amount of child support collections made on behalf of non-AFDC/TANF families for the year. The amount of a state's incentive payment could reach a maximum of 10% of the AFDC/TANF collections plus 10% of the non-AFDC/TANF collections, depending on the state's ratio of CSE collections to CSE expenditures. There was an additional limit (i.e., cap), however, on the incentive payment for non-AFDC/TANF collections. The incentive payment for such collections could not exceed 115% of incentive payments for AFDC/TANF collections. In addition, the old incentive payment system incorporated only one performance measure (i.e., cost-effectiveness) in determining incentive payments to states. One of the main criticisms of the old incentive payment system was that it did not provide an incentive for states to improve their programs because every state regardless of performance received the minimum incentive payment. There was general agreement by Congress that states whose CSE programs performed poorly should not be rewarded with federal funds.

[10] The CSE incentive payment system was fully implemented in FY2002.

[11] The incentive payment cap was $504 million in FY2009 and FY2010; $513 million in FY2011; $508 million in FY2012; and is estimated at $530 million for FY2013.

[12] In FY1998, the incentive payment, which at that time came out of the gross federal share of child support collected on behalf of TANF families, was $395 million. Beginning in FY2002, child support incentive payments were no longer paid out of the federal share of child support collections made on behalf of TANF families. Instead, federal funds have been specifically appropriated out of the U.S. Treasury for CSE incentive payments.

performance in five major areas. Instead of rewarding states only for their program's cost-effectiveness, the revised incentive payment system was designed to reward states for good performance in five different areas that were closely related to children obtaining child support payments (from their noncustodial parent). The revised incentive payment system was touted as one that would provide real incentives for the states to improve the CSE program, help families attain self-sufficiency, and support important societal goals like paternity identification and parental responsibility.[13]

P.L. 105-200 also revised the financial penalty system for the CSE program to reflect that improved performance is especially critical in three areas: paternity establishment, child support order establishment, and current child support collections. If specified performance standards are not met in these three areas, financial penalties through a reduction in the state's TANF block grant are imposed.

The revised/current CSE incentive payment system added an element of uncertainty to what used to be a somewhat predictable source of income for states. Although in the aggregate, states receive higher incentive payments than under the earlier incentive payment system, the total amount available is fixed (as noted in the previous section), and individual states have to compete with each other for their share of the capped funds. Under the revised incentive system, whether or not a state receives an incentive payment for good performance and the total amount of its incentive payment depends on several factors: the total amount of money available in a given fiscal year from which to make incentive payments, the state's success in obtaining collections on behalf of its caseload,[14] the state's performance in five areas (see text box below), the reliability of a state's data, and the relative success or failure of other states in making collections and meeting the performance criteria.

Moreover, unlike the old incentive system which allowed states and counties to spend incentive payments on whatever they chose, the current incentive payment system requires that the incentive payment be reinvested by the state into either the CSE program or some other activity which might lead to improving the efficiency or effectiveness of the CSE program (e.g., mediation/conflict-resolution services to parents, parenting classes, efforts to improve the earning capacity of noncustodial parents, etc.). Also, federal matching funds are no longer available to increase the value of incentive payments.

Calculation of State CSE Incentive Payments

The CSE incentive payment structure is very complex. For a fuller explanation of how state incentive payments are calculated, see the example given in the CSE FY2011 preliminary report.[15]

CSE incentive payments to states are based on several factors including state collections of child support payments and the performance of the states in five areas. The five performance measures are related to (1) establishment of paternity, (2) establishment of child support orders, (3) collection of current child support, (4) collection of child support arrearages (i.e., past-due child support), and (5) cost-effectiveness of the CSE program.

---

[13] Department of Health and Human Services. News Release. *HHS Submits Plan to Congress on New Rewards for States to Improve Child Support Collections.* March 13, 1997.

[14] The CSE program serves both welfare and nonwelfare families in its caseload. OCSE defines a CSE "case" as a noncustodial parent (mother, father, or putative/alleged father) who is now or eventually may be obligated under law for the support of a child or children receiving services under the CSE program. If the noncustodial parent owes support for two children by different women, that would be considered two cases; if both children have the same mother, that would be considered one case.

[15] Go to the following website and scroll nearly to the end of the document to the section entitled How an Incentive Payment is determined: http://www.acf.hhs.gov/programs/css/resource/fy2011-preliminary-report.

CSE Performance Measures

(1) Paternity Establishment. States have two options:

(A) CSE Paternity Establishment Percentage (PEP). State performance on paternity establishment is calculated by dividing the total number of children in the state's CSE caseload during the fiscal year (or at state option at the end of the fiscal year) who were born outside of marriage and for whom paternity has been established by the total number of children in the state's CSE caseload as of the end of the preceding fiscal year who were born outside of marriage;

(B) Statewide Paternity Establishment Percentage (PEP). State performance on paternity establishment is calculated by dividing the total number of minor children who were born outside of marriage and for whom paternity has been established during the fiscal year by the total number of children born outside of marriage during the preceding fiscal year.

(2) Establishment of Child Support Orders. State performance on support orders is calculated by dividing the number of cases in the CSE caseload for which there is a support order by the total number of cases in the program.

(3) Current Payments. State performance on current payments is obtained by dividing the total dollars collected for current support in cases in the CSE caseload by the total amount owed on support in these cases which is not past-due.

(4) Arrearage Payments. State performance on arrears (i.e., past-due payments) is obtained by dividing the number of cases in which there was some payment on arrearages during the fiscal year by the total number of cases in which past-due support is owed. (Cases in which the family was formerly on welfare, and in which arrearages are collected by federal income tax intercept, do not count as an arrearage payment case unless the state shares the collection with the family.)

(5) Cost-Effectiveness. State performance on cost-effectiveness is determined by dividing the total amount collected through the child support program by the total amount spent by the program to make these collections.

Under the CSE incentive payment system, each of the five performance measures is translated into a mathematical formula (see text box that follows). The amount of incentive payments for a particular performance measure is based on a standard that is specified in law. For each performance standard, there is an upper threshold. All states that achieve performance levels at or above this upper threshold are entitled to the maximum possible incentive for that performance measure. Simultaneously, there is also a minimum level of performance below which states do not receive an incentive, unless the state makes significant improvement over its previous year's performance.

To determine a state's incentive payment, the following computations must be made. First, each state's performance percentage for each performance measure is separately determined and translated into the applicable percentage for that particular

Performance Thresholds (and applicable percentage)

If PEP	≥ 80%, then 100%	if < 50%, then 0%
If order establishment	≥ 80%, then 100%	if < 50%, then 0%
If current support	≥ 80%, then 100%	if < 40%, then 0%
If arrearages	≥ 80%, then 100%	if < 40%, then 0%
If cost-effectiveness	≥ 5.00, then 100%	if < 2.00, then 0%

performance measure. If the performance percentage is at or above the upper threshold, the applicable percentage for that performance measure would be 100%. If the performance percentage is below the lower threshold, the applicable percentage for that performance measure would be 0%.[16] If the performance percentage is in between these two points (the upper and lower thresholds), the applicable percentage is obtained by referring to the tables specified in federal law (Section 458(b)(6) of the Social Security Act) for each of the performance measures. For example, with regard to the establishment of

---

[16] At the low end of the performance scale, there is a minimum level below which a state is not rewarded with an incentive payment unless the state demonstrates a substantial improvement over the prior year's performance. Even though substantial improvement is recognized, the law stipulates that the incentive payment in such cases cannot exceed 50% of the maximum incentive possible for that performance measure. The substantial improvement provisions do not apply with respect to the cost-effectiveness performance measure.

child support orders, if the state's performance percentage for this measure is 70%, meaning that 70% of CSE cases in the state have a child support order, the applicable percentage is 80%.

Second, after the applicable percentage for each performance measure is determined, that percentage is multiplied by the "collections" base for an individual state. The collections base is calculated by using the following formula: [2 x (current assistance collections + former assistance collections + Medicaid never assistance collections)+ never on TANF collections + fees retained by other states].[17]

Third, if the performance measure is paternity establishment, child support order establishment, or current collections, then the resulting amount (i.e., the applicable percentage multiplied by the collections base) is multiplied by 100%. If the performance measure is past-due collections (i.e., arrearages) or cost-effectiveness, then the resulting amount is multiplied by 75%. These calculations result in maximum incentives for each performance measure.

Fourth, the maximum incentives are added together. The dollar amount that is obtained by adding together the five maximum incentives for each performance measure is called the maximum incentive base amount.

Fifth, all of the states' (includes the four jurisdictions: the District of Columbia, Guam, Puerto Rico, and the Virgin Islands) maximum incentive base amounts are then added together for a total maximum incentive base amount.

Sixth, each state's individual maximum base amount is compared to the total maximum incentive base amount. The mathematical formula would be—maximum state incentive base/sum of all state incentive bases. An individual state's share of the total is the percentage that is used to determine the state's actual incentive payment. For example, if a state's share of the total is 17%, then the state will receive 17% of the capped incentive payment for the fiscal year in question. In FY2011 for example, the state's incentive payment would be $87,210,000 (.17* $513 million).

The federal government makes incentive payments to states on an on-going quarterly prospective basis using state *estimates* of what their incentive payments will total. After the audited performance data (discussed below) are available, OCSE reconciles the incentive payment actually earned with the amount previously estimated, and received, by the state.[18]

Data Reliability

Before enactment of P.L. 105-200, incentive payments (under the old system) were not dependent on data reliability. Although audits were performed at least once every three years to ensure compliance with federal CSE program requirements, the audits were focused on administrative procedures and processes rather than performance outcomes and results.

---

[17] It was decided during the negotiations on revising the incentive payment system that, because collecting child support on behalf of TANF and former-TANF families is generally more difficult than collecting child support on behalf of families who had never been on TANF, the incentive formula should provide a greater emphasis on collection in TANF and former TANF cases. Moreover, it was mentioned that collections in TANF cases provide direct savings to the state and federal governments. The incentive payment formula thus doubles the collections made on behalf of TANF and former-TANF cases to give them extra emphasis. (See Office of Child Support Enforcement, Department of Health and Human Services. *Child Support Enforcement Incentive Funding*. Report to the House Ways and Means Committee and the Senate Finance Committee. February 1997. p. 8.)

[18] 45 C.F. R. §305.34. Also see Office of Child Support Enforcement, *Data Reliability Audit Requirements for the Fiscal Year 2011 Reporting Period*, Dear Colleague Letter-DCL-11-15, August 22, 2011.

Under current federal law, states are accountable for providing reliable data on a timely basis or they receive no incentive payments. The data reliability provisions were enacted as part of P.L. 105-200, which established the current incentive payment system. They are in the law to ensure the integrity of the incentive payment system. The federal Office of Child Support Enforcement (OCSE) Office of Audit performs data reliability audits to evaluate the completeness, accuracy, security, and reliability of data reported and produced by state reporting systems. The audits help ensure that incentives under the Child Support Performance and Incentives Act of 1998 (P.L. 105-200) are earned and paid only on the basis of verifiable data and that the incentive payments system is fair and equitable. If an audit determines that a state's data are not complete and reliable for a given performance measure, the state receives zero payments for that measure[19] and are subject to federal financial penalties. Although estimated incentive payments are sent to states on a prospective quarterly basis, those estimated incentive payments are reconciled to the actual incentive payment earned after the auditing process. Thus, if a state fails the audit on a particular performance measure, the state would not receive an incentive payment for that measure (i.e., the state's funding would be reduced to reflect the audit's findings).[20]

The audit for the fiscal year generally begins at the beginning of a calendar year (after the fiscal year has ended) and is completed by early summer.[21] States provide the assigned regional OCSE office with a universe of cases and audit trails. From this universe, a sample is selected. The auditor selects at least 150 cases from the state's universe. States are required to provide auditors with documentation, through access to state computerized/automated systems and hard copies of documents for each of the sample cases. The auditor reviews the sample cases to determine if the items he or she is trying to verify are correct. For example, if the documentation indicates that $450 in current support was paid during the fiscal year, the auditor looks up the collection history for that particular case on the state's automated system to determine if the $450 figure is correct. Federal regulations (Title 45 CFR Section 305.1(i)) require data to meet a 95% standard of reliability.[22] Once the audit is completed, the general practice is for an auditor from a different field office to review the findings. Moreover, the OCSE headquarters staff that work on audits also review audit findings. Informational sessions and opportunities to contest the findings are available to states during the audit process.[23]

---

[19] According to the most recent published data, 51 states/territories passed the data reliability audits for FY2009 (the names of the states/territories that passed and did not pass the audit were not published). Source: U.S. Department of Health and Human Services. Administration for Children and Families, Office of Child Support Enforcement, *Office of Child Support Enforcement FY 2009 Annual Report to Congress*. December 2009—http://www.acf.hhs.gov/programs/css/resource/fy2009-annual-report, p. 12.

[20] According to the federal regulations (45 CFR Part 304.12): Each state calculates the federal government's share of child support payments collected on behalf of TANF families. Then the state retains one-fourth of its annual estimate of incentive payments from the federal government's share of child support collected on behalf of TANF families each quarter. Following the end of a fiscal year, the OCSE will calculate the actual incentive payment the state should have received based on the reports submitted for that fiscal year. If adjustments to the estimate are necessary, the state's quarterly TANF grant award will be reduced or increased because of over- or under-estimates for prior quarters and for other adjustments.

[21] Thereby, the audit of FY2011 (October 1, 2010-September 30, 2011) incentive payment data would usually begin in January 2011 and generally would be completed by July 2011. Once the audit is completed, estimated incentive payments would be reconciled with actual incentive payments.

[22] Title 45 CFR Section 305.1(i) states that " ... data may contain errors as long as they are not of a magnitude that would cause a reasonable person, aware of the errors, to doubt a finding or conclusion based on the data."

[23] *Study of the Implementation of the Performance-Based Incentive System—Interim Report*, by the Lewin Group (Karen Gardiner, Michael Fishman, and Asaph Glosser) and ECONorthwest (John Tapogna). Prepared for the Office of Child Support Enforcement. October 2003. p. 14.

Federal Financial Penalties

The CSE performance-based penalty system provides that a financial penalty be assessed when data submitted for calculating state performance are found to be incomplete or unreliable. Penalties may also be assessed when the calculated level of performance for any of three performance measures—paternity establishment, support order establishment, or current collections—fails to achieve a specified level or when states are not in compliance with certain child support requirements.

There is an automatic corrective action year if performance measures and data reliability are not achieved. The corrective action year is the immediately succeeding fiscal year following the year of the deficiency. If the state's data are determined complete and reliable and the related performance is adequate for the corrective action year, the penalty is not imposed.

If the corrective action was unsuccessful, the financial penalty is a reduction in the state's TANF block grant. Historically, Congress has linked the CSE program and the TANF (and old AFDC) program. Currently Section 402(a)(2) of the Social Security Act (Title IV-A which deals with TANF (and used to pertain to the AFDC program)) stipulates that the governor of a state must certify that it will operate an approved CSE program as a condition of receiving TANF block grant funding. Since the enactment of the CSE program in 1975, there has always been a provision in federal law that linked poor performance (and penalties) or noncompliance in the CSE program with a reduction in Title IV-A funding.

Under the performance-based audit procedures (Section 409(a)(8) of the Social Security Act), a graduated penalty equal to 1%-5% of the federal TANF block grant is assessed against a state if (1) on the basis of the data submitted by the state for a review, the state CSE program fails to achieve the paternity establishment or other performance standards set by the HHS Secretary;[24] (2) an audit finds that the state data are incomplete or unreliable; or (3) the state failed to substantially comply with one or more CSE state plan requirements, and the state fails to correct the deficiencies in the fiscal year following the performance year (i.e., the corrective action plan year).

The penalty amount is calculated as not less than 1% nor more than 2% of the TANF block grant program for the first year of the deficiency. The penalty amount increases each year, up to 5%,[25] for each consecutive year the state's data are found to be incomplete, unreliable, or the state's performance on a penalty measure fails to attain the specified level of performance. According to the CSE annual data report for FY2010: "One state showed a deficiency related to the PEP and will have one corrective action year to correct the deficiency."[26]

---

[24] There are three performance measures for which states have to achieve certain levels of performance in order to avoid being penalized for poor performance. These measures are (1) paternity establishment [specifically mentioned in the federal law— Section 409(a)(8)(A) of the Social Security Act], (2) child support order establishment, and (3) current child support collections [these last two performance measures were designated by the HHS Secretary—45 CFR Section 305.40].

[25] The penalty amount is calculated as not less than 2% nor more than 3% of the TANF block grant program for the second year of the deficiency. The penalty amount is calculated as not less than 3% nor more than 5% of the TANF block grant program for the third or subsequent year of the deficiency.

[26] U.S. Department of Health and Human Services, Administration for Children and Families, Office of Child Support Enforcement, *Child Support Enforcement Annual Report to Congress FY2010*, April 12, 2013, p. 12. Note that published data related to penalties usually are in CSE's Annual Report to Congress. The most recent annual report is for FY2010. Although the preliminary data report for FY2011 is available (published), it does not contain data related to audits or penalties.

State Trends

A state's share of incentive payments depends on many factors that are distinct to its population and CSE caseload. CSE collection can be straightforward. In most CSE cases paternity has already been established and in a majority of cases the child support order was established at the time of the divorce or separation. Further, many noncustodial parents are up-to-date in their child support payments and do not owe any past-due (arrearage) payments. However, in other cases meeting CSE performance measures can be more difficult. Although not exactly sequential, the CSE performance measures are very interdependent. A child support order cannot be established if paternity has not been legally determined. Child support payments cannot be collected or enforced unless a child support order has been established. Arrearage payments cannot be collected if current child support is not paid. States that have more cases that require services such as paternity establishment, child support order establishment, and payment of arrearages generally have a tougher time collecting child support than states that do not face such challenges.

In FY2011, the aggregate incentive payment amount was $513 million. Among the 50 states and the 4 jurisdictions of the District of Columbia, Guam, Puerto Rico, and the Virgin Islands, CSE incentive payments in FY2011 ranged from a high of $59.6 million in Texas to a low of $77,575 in the Virgin Islands.[27]

As mentioned earlier, incentive payments are a function of a state's collections base, which is largely dependent on population size. Thus, the aggregate amount of incentive dollars received by individual states is a poor indicator of a state's performance with respect to individual performance measures. As discussed in more detail later, incentive payments are not directly correlated with performance. In other words, even though a state may receive a high incentive payment, the state's performance on one or several individual performance measures may be very poor. This results because child support collections are the critical determinant of incentive payments to states. In fact, the top seven states with regard to collecting child support were the top seven states with regard to high incentive payments in both FY2002 and FY2011 (and throughout much of the period in between).[28]

Performance Incentive Scores

The data presented in this report are based on the unaudited incentive payment performance scores. These data are readily available each year when OCSE publishes its preliminary data report. Over the years, states have made significant improvement in the area of data reliability. According to the final report on FY2009 data, only three jurisdictions failed data reliability audits.

A comparison of FY2002 performance score data to FY2011 performance score data[29] shows that CSE program performance has improved with respect to all five performance measures. The following scores represent the total score for all 54 jurisdictions for each of the performance measures (referred to in this analysis as national averages). The national average for the paternity establishment score went from 73%

---

[27] The OCSE has not yet published actual incentive payment data by state for FY2012.

[28] In FY2002, the states with the highest incentive payments were California, Texas, Pennsylvania, New York, Michigan, Florida, and New Jersey. In FY2011, the states with the highest incentive payments were Texas, California, Florida, New York, Pennsylvania, Ohio, Michigan, and New Jersey. These states also are the most populous states.

[29] The table for the FY2002 data can be found at http://www.acf.dhhs.gov/programs/cse/pubs/2003/reports/prelim_datareport/. The table for the FY2011 data can be found at http://www.acf.hhs.gov/programs/css/resource/fy2011-preliminary-report-table-p-35.

(CSE program measure rather than statewide measure) in FY2002 to 99% in FY2011; the score for child support order establishment increased from 70% to 81%; the score for current child support collections increased from 58% to 62%; the score for child support arrearage cases increased from 60% to 62%; and the cost-effectiveness score increased from 4.13 to 5.12.

Table 1. Child Support Enforcement Performance Incentive Scores: National Averages (Selected Years)

Performance Measures	FY2002	FY2005	FY2010	FY2011
CSE Paternity Establishment Percentage	72.62	87.57	97.26	98.96
Child Support Order Establishment Score	70.40	75.87	80.02	80.92
Current Child Support Collections Score	57.55	59.91	61.96	62.44
Child Support Arrearage Cases Score	59.56	60.04	61.98	62.17
Cost-Effectiveness Score	4.13	4.58	4.88	5.12

Source: U.S. Department of Health and Human Services, Office of Child Support Enforcement, Preliminary Data Reports for the Selected Years.

The following analysis examines the individual CSE performance measures for the years FY2002, FY2005, FY2010, and FY2011. It focuses on the median,[30] maximum, and minimum scores for all five performance measures. The median score sometimes better illustrates trends because unlike the mean (i.e., average) it is not affected by very high or very low scores.

Paternity Establishment Percentage (PEP)

One of the goals of the CSE program has always been to establish paternity for those needing that service. In fact the official title of the program when it was enacted in 1975 and to this day is Child Support and Establishment of Paternity. The CSE program's strategic plan for FY2005-FY2009[31] reiterated this by indicating that goal #1 of the program is that all children have an established parentage and the program tries to achieve this goal by increasing the percentage of children with a legal relationship with their parents.

As mentioned earlier in the CSE performance measures text box, states have two options for determining the Paternity Establishment Percentage (PEP). They can use a PEP that is based on data that pertain solely to the CSE program or they can use a PEP that is based on data that pertain to the state population as a whole. In effect, the PEP compares paternities established during the fiscal year with the number of nonmarital births during the preceding fiscal year. This calculation permits scores to exceed 100%. A PEP of 100% or more generally means that the state has established paternity for more than just the newborns

---

[30] The median reflects the performance of the middle-ranked state (i.e., the 27th state in rank order), with all states weighted equally.

[31] Although a strategic plan for subsequent and future years has been drafted, the enactment of the Affordable Care Act (P.L. 111-148), technological advances, and resource contraints have resulted in ongoing discussions among interested parties in the CSE program about the future of the program.

who were born outside of marriage in the specified year (i.e., the state has established paternity for many older children as well).[32]

The median PEP score among the 54 jurisdictions[33] with CSE programs was 86.64 in FY2002, 91.47 in FY2005, 94.69 in FY2010, and 97.32 in FY2011. The maximum PEP score was 130.75 in FY2002, it rose to 112.42 in FY2005, 118.29 in FY2010, and 126.33 in FY2011. The minimum PEP score started at 50.83 in FY2002, increased to 54.05 in FY2005 and to 81.26 in FY2010, and then dropped to 77.98 in FY2011.

According to the CSE FY2010 Annual Report:

> Feedback from the field continues to suggest that states are facing greater challenges to maintain the high performance levels. At the time the incentive/penalty structure began, states had a backlog of cases that enabled them to exceed the 90 percent performance level for PEP. However, with the maturation of the system and the declining birth rate, many states have reduced or even eliminated their backlog of cases for establishing paternity. Normal annual variations in performance (91 percent rate one year, 89 percent the next) can result in a substantial penalty without indicating operational or performance problems. While the number of states currently receiving a penalty is still low, we believe that, in the future, more and more states will find it difficult to achieve the current acceptable performance level and will allocate a disproportionate amount of resources to this function in an attempt to stay out of penalty status.[34]

---

[32] As mentioned earlier in the text box, a state may use as its PEP either the CSE PEP or the statewide PEP. The state CSE PEP is based on the entire number of children in the CSE caseload who had been born outside of marriage, regardless of year of birth, and whether paternity had been established for them. If the CSE PEP is more than 100%, then the number of children on the CSE rolls who were born outside of marriage but had paternity established on their behalf exceeded the number of children on the CSE rolls who were born outside of marriage in any previous year. Whereas, if the statewide PEP is more than 100%, then the number of paternities established in the current fiscal year exceeded the number of babies born outside of marriage in the preceding fiscal year.

[33] According to preliminary FY2002 data, Guam had the maximum PEP score of 452.87, but that score for Guam was excluded because of conflicting data.

[34] U.S. Department of Health and Human Services, Administration for Children and Families, Office of Child Support Enforcement, *Child Support Enforcement Annual Report to Congress FY2010*, April 12, 2013, pp. 11-12.

Figure 1. Paternity Establishment Scores: Maximum, Median, Minimum (Selected Years)

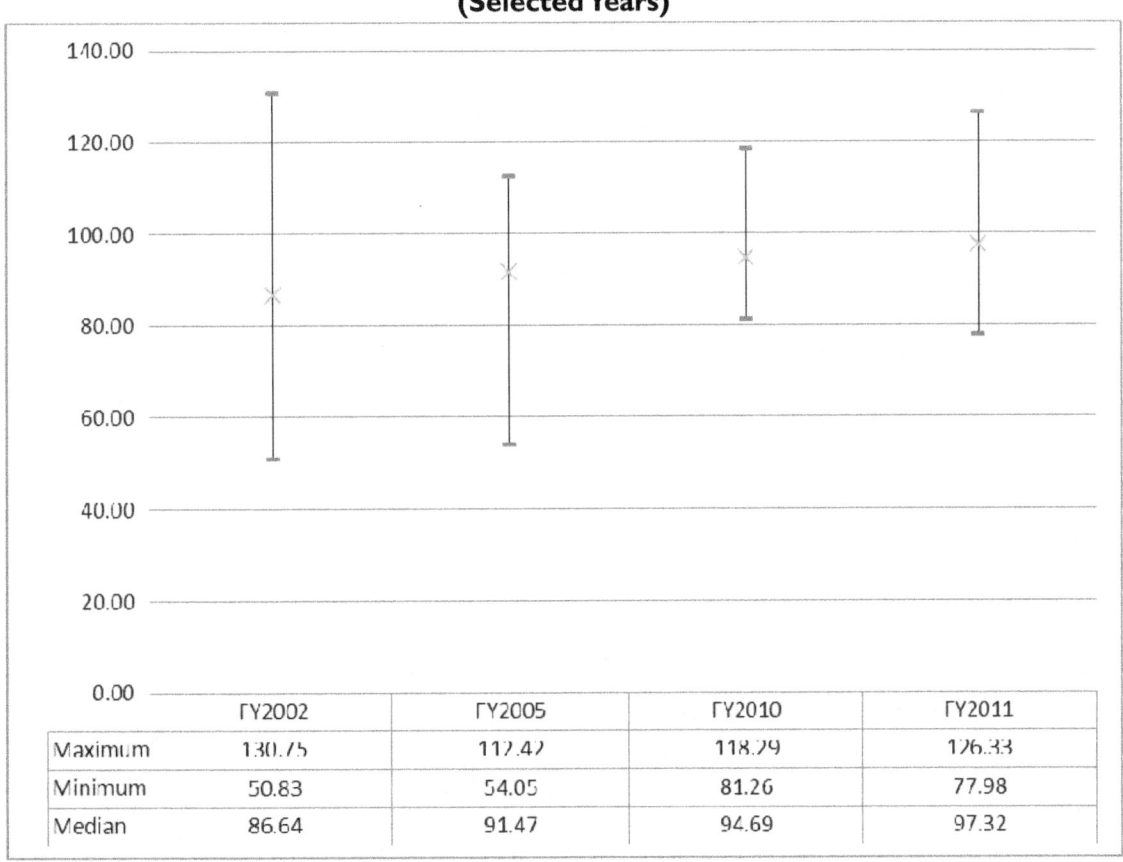

	ΓY2002	ΓY2005	ΓY2010	ΓY2011
Maximum	130.75	112.42	118.29	126.33
Minimum	50.83	54.05	81.26	77.98
Median	86.64	91.47	94.69	97.32

Source: Chart prepared by the Congressional Research Service based on data from the Office of Child Support Enforcement, Department of Health and Human Services.

Note: The x on the line graphs highlights the median score. In FY2002, on the basis of preliminary data, Guam had the maximum score (452.87). However, because of other conflicting data for Guam, that outlier PEP for Guam was excluded from this analysis. The next highest PEP score in FY2002 was 130.75 (Idaho).

Child Support Order Establishment Percentage

Goal #2 in the FY2005-FY2009 Strategic Plan of the Child Support Enforcement Program is for all children in the CSE caseload to have child support orders. The second performance measure focuses on the percentage of CSE cases that have a child support order (i.e., a legally-binding document that requires the noncustodial parent to pay child support).

The median child support order establishment score among the 54 jurisdictions with CSE programs rose in each of the years displayed, starting at 71.28 in FY2002 and ending at 82.90 in FY2011. The maximum score for this performance measure fluctuated; it started at 92.03 in FY2002, increased to 96.00 in FY2005, decreased to 92.38 in FY2010, and increased to 93.06 in FY2011. The minimum score for child support order establishment rose during the displayed years, starting at 29.66 in FY2002 and ending at 58.54 in FY2011.

Figure 2. Child Support Order Establishment Scores: Maximum, Median, Minimum (Selected Years)

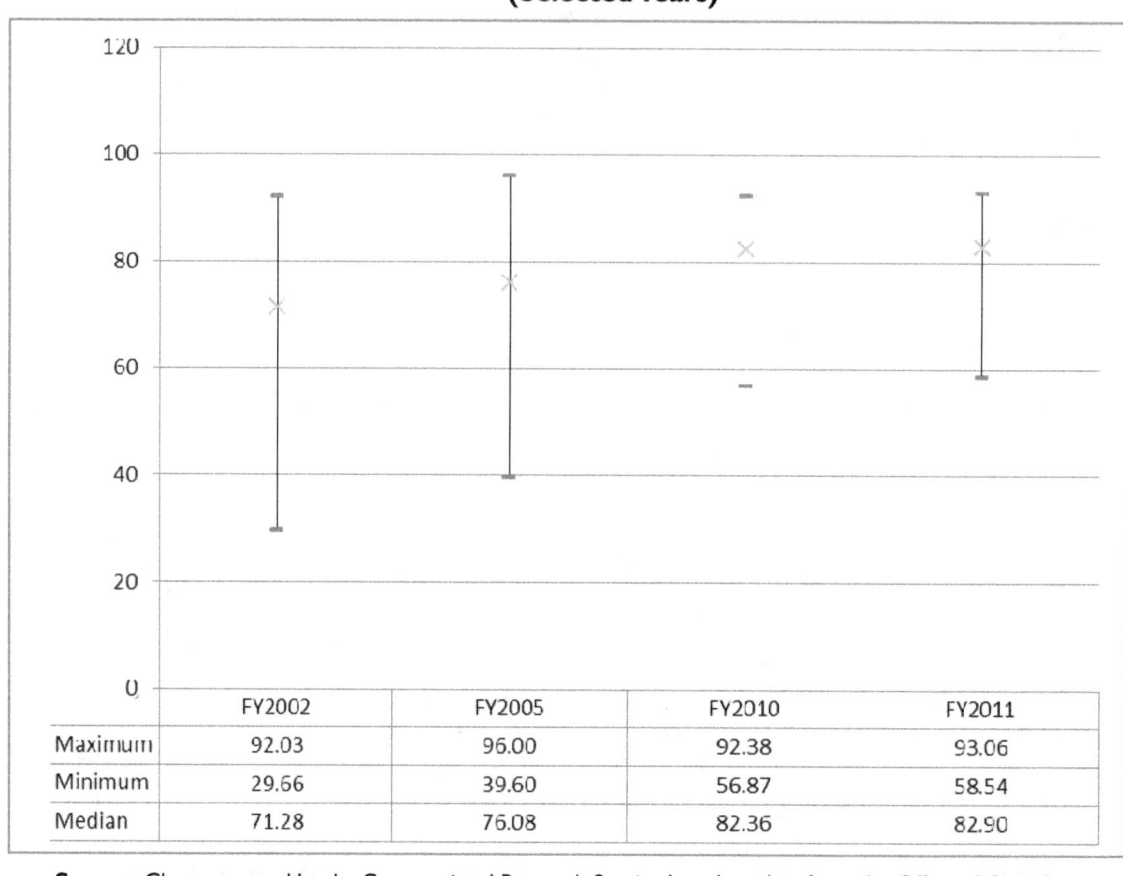

	FY2002	FY2005	FY2010	FY2011
Maximum	92.03	96.00	92.38	93.06
Minimum	29.66	39.60	56.87	58.54
Median	71.28	76.08	82.36	82.90

Source: Chart prepared by the Congressional Research Service based on data from the Office of Child Support Enforcement, Department of Health and Human Services.

Note: The x on the line graphs highlights the median score.

Current Child Support Collections Scores

Goal #4[35] in the FY2005-FY2009 Strategic Plan of the Child Support Enforcement Program is for all children in the CSE caseload to receive the financial support owed by their noncustodial parents. This goal encompasses both current child support payments and past-due child support payments (i.e., arrearages). The third performance indicator measures the proportion of current child support owed that is collected on behalf of children in the CSE caseload.

The median child support current collections score among the 54 jurisdictions with CSE programs was 57.10 in FY2002, 58.89 in FY2005, 60.80 in FY2010, and remained relatively unchanged in FY2011 (60.79). The maximum score was 74.70 in FY2002 and 83.90 in FY2011. The minimum score increased from 39.11 in FY2002 to 50.97 in FY2011.

---

[35] Goal #3 in the FY2005-FY2009 Strategic Plan of the CSE Program is for all children in the CSE program to have medical coverage.

Figure 3. Child Support Current Collections Scores: Maximum, Median, Minimum (Selected Years)

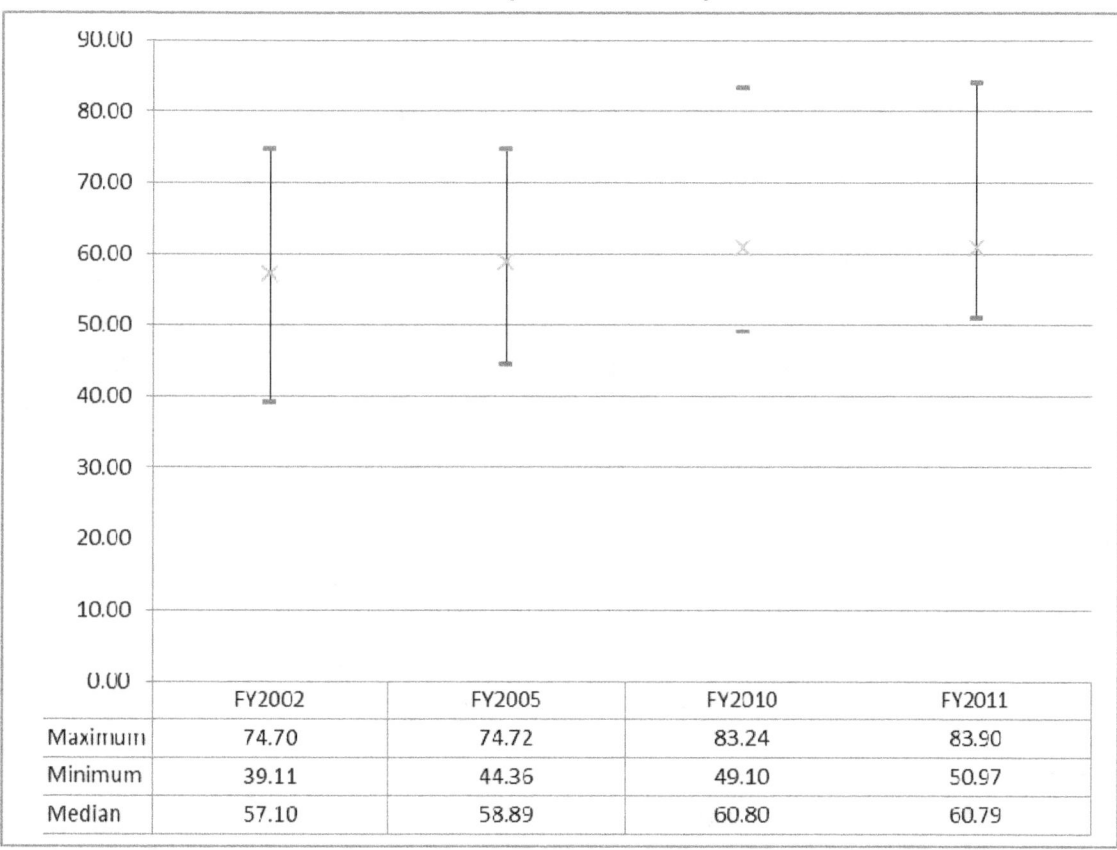

	FY2002	FY2005	FY2010	FY2011
Maximum	74.70	74.72	83.24	83.90
Minimum	39.11	44.36	49.10	50.97
Median	57.10	58.89	60.80	60.79

Source: Chart prepared by the Congressional Research Service based on data from the Office of Child Support Enforcement, Department of Health and Human Services.

Note: The x on the line graphs highlights the median score.

Child Support Arrearage Cases Scores

The fourth performance indicator measures state efforts to collect money from CSE cases with an arrearage (i.e., past-due child support payments are owed). This performance measure specifically counts paying cases—and not total arrearage dollars collected—because states have different methods of handling certain aspects of arrearage cases. For example, the ability to write off debt that is deemed uncollectible varies by state. Moreover, some states charge interest on arrearages (which is considered additional arrearages) while other states do not.[36] As mentioned above, this performance measure is incorporated in goal #4 as listed in the FY2005-FY2009 CSE Strategic Plan.

The median child support arrearage cases score among the 54 jurisdictions with CSE programs fluctuated during the years displayed. It was 60.71 in FY2002, 60.59 in FY2005, and 61.57 in both FY2010 and FY2011. The maximum score increased from 71.58 in FY2002 to 83.77 in FY2011. The minimum score rose from 30.21 in FY2002, increased to 45.61 in FY2010, and then declined to 45.37 in FY2011.

---

[36] *Interest on Past-Due Child Support*, http://www.supportguidelines.com/articles/art200301.html.

Figure 4. Child Support Arrearage Cases Scores: Maximum, Median, Minimum (Selected Years)

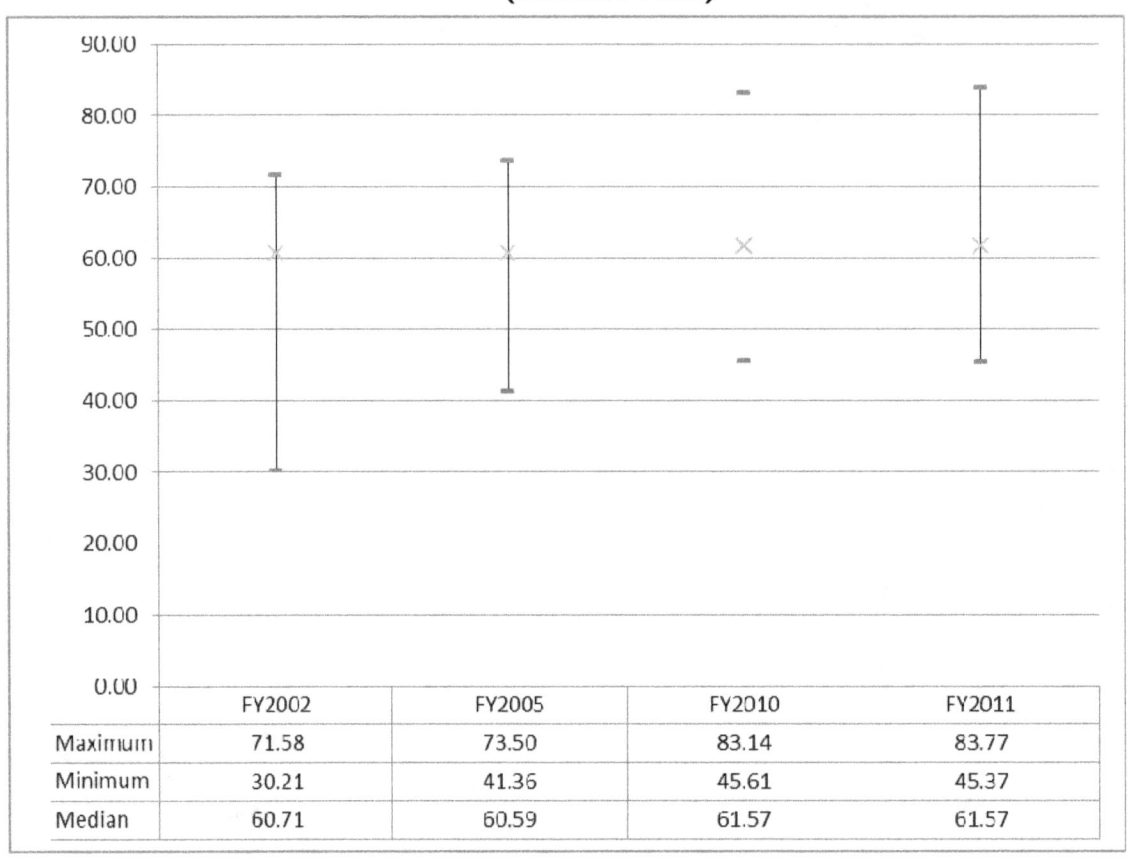

	FY2002	FY2005	FY2010	FY2011
Maximum	71.58	73.50	83.14	83.77
Minimum	30.21	41.36	45.61	45.37
Median	60.71	60.59	61.57	61.57

Source: Chart prepared by the Congressional Research Service based on data from the Office of Child Support Enforcement, Department of Health and Human Services.

Note: The x on the line graphs highlights the median score.

Cost-Effectiveness Scores

Goal #5 in the FY2005-FY2009 Strategic Plan of the Child Support Enforcement Program says that the CSE program will be efficient and responsive in its operations. The fifth performance measure assesses the total dollars collected by the CSE program for each dollar spent.

The median cost-effectiveness score among the 54 jurisdictions with CSE programs for the years displayed was 4.49 in FY2002, it rose to 4.77 in FY2005, then fell to 4.69 in FY2010, and increased to 5.30 in FY2011. The maximum score went from 7.80 in FY2002 to 12.54 in FY2010, and then dropped to 10.41 in FY2011. The minimum score was 1.46 in FY2002, reached 2.10 in FY2005, then dropped to 1.42 in FY2010, and increased to 1.98 in FY2011.

According to the CSE Annual Report for FY2010, "*Increases in this measure stem mainly from declines in state program expenditures due to funding shortfalls compared to collections that have not declined to the same extent, but have remained flat.*"[37]

---

[37] U.S. Department of Health and Human Services, Administration for Children and Families, Office of Child Support Enforcement, *Child Support Enforcement Annual Report to Congress FY2010*, April 12, 2013, p. 12.

Figure 5. Cost-Effectiveness Scores: Maximum, Median, Minimum (Selected Years)

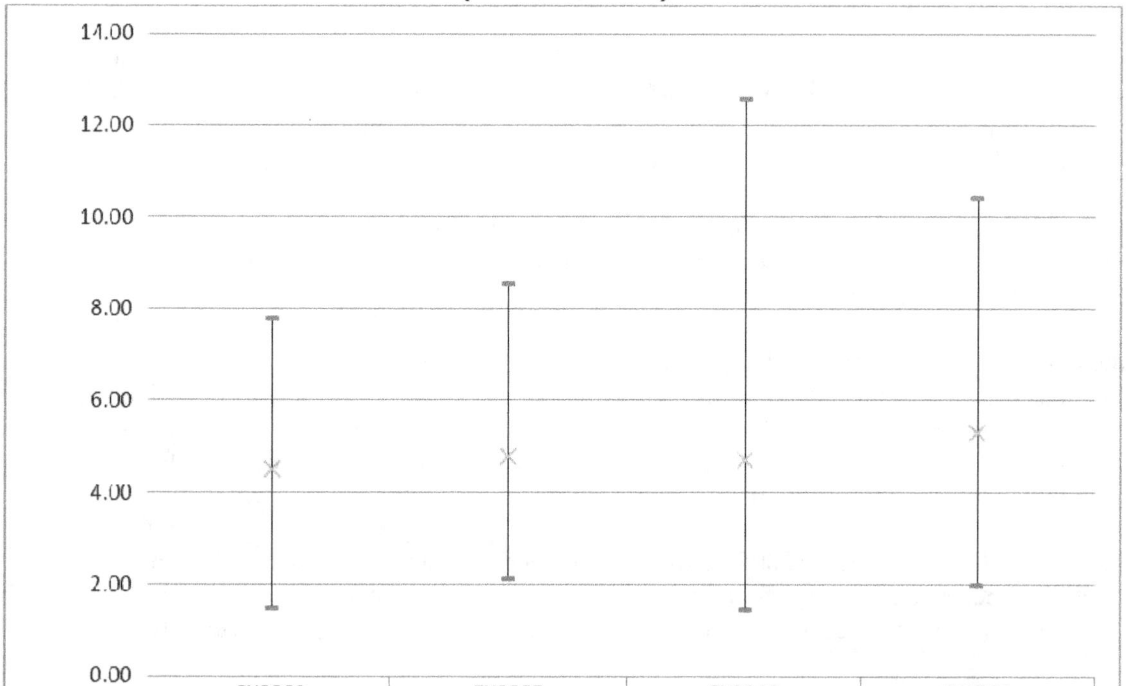

	FY2002	FY2005	FY2010	FY2011
Maximum	7.80	8.53	12.54	10.41
Minimum	1.46	2.10	1.42	1.98
Median	4.49	4.77	4.69	5.30

Source: Chart prepared by the Congressional Research Service based on data from the Office of Child Support Enforcement, Department of Health and Human Services.

Note: The x on the line graphs highlights the median score.

Incentive Payments for All Performance Measures

Although CSE incentive payments were awarded to all 54 jurisdictions (including the 50 states, the District of Columbia, Guam, Puerto Rico, and the Virgin Islands) in FY2002, FY2005, FY2010, and FY2011, some jurisdictions performed poorly on certain performance measures and thereby did not receive an incentive for that measure. (See the earlier text box on performance thresholds for the percentage scores on each performance measure that do not warrant an incentive payment.) The 54 jurisdictions (in aggregate) improved their performance over the selected years. In FY2002, 46 jurisdictions received an incentive for all five performance measures compared to 53 jurisdictions in FY2005, FY2010, and FY2011.

On the basis of the unaudited FY2002 performance incentive scores of the 54 jurisdictions, 46 jurisdictions received an incentive for all five performance measures, 3 jurisdictions received an incentive for four performance measures (California, Hawaii, and Mississippi), and 5 jurisdictions (Illinois, New Mexico, the District of Columbia, Guam, and the Virgin Islands) received an incentive for three performance measures. (See **Table B-2**.)

On the basis of the unaudited FY2005 performance incentive scores of the 54 jurisdictions, 53 jurisdictions received an incentive for all five performance measures and the remaining jurisdiction (the District of Columbia) received an incentive for four performance measures. (See **Table B-3**.)

On the basis of the unaudited FY2010 performance incentive scores of the 54 jurisdictions, 53 jurisdictions received an incentive for all five performance measures, and 1 jurisdiction received an incentive for four performance measures (the Virgin Islands). (See **Table B-4**.)

On the basis of the unaudited FY2011 performance incentive scores of the 54 jurisdictions, 53 jurisdictions received an incentive for all five performance measures, and 1 jurisdiction received an incentive for four performance measures (the Virgin Islands). (See **Table B-5**.)

Relationship Between Incentive Payments and Performance Measures

Given that the incentive payment is based on five performance measures, it is likely that all jurisdictions would continue to receive some amount of incentive payments. However, if individual performance measures are examined, a different picture develops; some states may not perform well enough to receive an incentive payment with respect to one of the five performance measures. **Table B-2**, **Table B-3**, **Table B-4**, and **Table B-5** show the five performance measures by state (includes jurisdictions) for each of the four selected years (FY2002, FY2005, FY2010, and FY2011).[38] The states in each of the tables are ranked from highest performing state (relative to each indicator) to lowest performing state. These tables illustrate that the relationship between actual performance and CSE incentive payments is not always transparent. That is, even though a state may receive a high incentive payment, the state's performance on one or several individual performance measures may be very poor.

Child support collections are a very important component in determining the amount of a state's incentive payment. As mentioned earlier, incentive payments are a function of a state's collections base, which is composed of child support collected on behalf of current and former TANF families multiplied by two

---

[38] OCSE has not yet published data showing the incentive payments received by states in FY2012.

plus the collection amount made on behalf of families who have never been on TANF.[39] The main reason that there is not a more direct relationship between incentive payments and performance levels is that the incentive payment calculation is so heavily dependent on child support collections. The prominence of child support collections in the incentive payment formula results in the more populous states receiving the largest incentive payments.

Thus, a high collections base can mean that a state receives a high incentive payment despite low performance measures. For example, although California received the highest incentive payment in FY2002 and FY2005 and the second highest incentive payment in FY2010 and FY2011,[40] it ranked very low with regard to cost-effectiveness (51st in FY2002 and FY2005, 52nd in FY2010, and 51st in FY2011). However, because California collected substantially more child support payments than the next ranking state (21% more in FY2011) and because most of those collections were on behalf of TANF or former-TANF families (63% in FY2011), it is not surprising that California received the highest amount of incentive payments in FY2002 and FY2005 and the second highest amount in FY2010 and FY2011.[41] According to OCSE annual data reports, the top seven states with regard to collecting child support (in FY2002, FY2005, FY2010, and FY2011) were the top seven states with regard to high incentive payments (although not in the same rank order).

Policy Issues

The current performance-based incentive payment system is part of the CSE program's strategic plan to set goals and measure results. Despite a general consensus that the CSE program is doing well, questions still arise about whether the program is effectively meeting its mission and concerns exist over whether the program will be able to meet future expectations in light of reductions in federal funding that were made pursuant to the Deficit Reduction Act of 2005 (P.L. 109-171).

Some in the CSE "community" (e.g., states, CSE workers, analysts, state policymakers, and advocates) contend that several factors may cause a state not to receive an incentive payment that is commensurate with its relative performance on individual measures. These factors include static or declining CSE collections; sliding scale performance scores that financially benefit states at the upper end (but not the top) of the artificial threshold and financially disadvantage states at the lower end of the artificial threshold; a limited number of performance indicators that do not encompass all of the components critical to a successful CSE program; and a statutory maximum on the aggregate amount of incentive payments that can be paid to states—which causes states to have to compete with each other for their share of the capped funds.

Others point out that the current CSE incentive payment system was developed with much thought and input from the CSE community. They maintain that the incentive payment formula rewards states for their

---

[39] Pursuant to §458(b)(5)(C) of the Social Security Act, a state's collections base = 2 x (TANF collections + Formerly on TANF collections) + Never on TANF collections + Fees retained by other states.

[40] Texas was ranked second highest with regard to incentive payments in FY2002 and FY2005 and highest in FY2010 and FY2011.

[41] California collected 31% more in child support payments than Texas in FY2002 and 25% more in child support payments than Texas in FY2005. Texas collected 32% more in child support payments than California in FY2010 and 44% more in FY2011. Given that the incentive formula gives more weight to child support collections made on behalf of TANF and former-TANF families than on families that have never been on TANF, it is important to note that the majority of the child support collected in California for the four years displayed was on behalf of TANF and former-TANF families. Specifically, in FY2002, FY2005, FY2010, and FY2011, 75%, 65%, 63%, and 63% (respectively) of CSE collections in California were made on behalf of TANF and former-TANF families. The comparable figures for Texas are: 59%, 59%, 54%, and 54%.

performance in five critical areas, consistent with the legislated mission of the CSE program as well as the program's strategic plan and related outcome measures. They say that the performance thresholds were designed to provide tough but reachable targets for performance by rewarding states with higher incentives as they improve. In addition, it is argued that the annual cap on incentive payments (imposed by P.L. 105-200) has encouraged competition among the states and that there is no evidence that the cap has stifled the motivation of states to improve performance.

This section discusses the following list of issues: (1) "Does the CSE Incentive Payment System Reward Good Performance?" (2)"Should Incentive Payments Be Based on Additional Performance Indicators?" (3) "Should TANF Funds Be Reduced Because of Poor CSE Performance?" (4) "Why Aren't the Incentives and Penalties Consistent for the Paternity Establishment Performance Measure?" (5) "Should Incentive Payments Be Based on Individual State Performance Rather Than Aggregate State Performance?" and (6) "Will the Elimination of the Federal Match of Incentive Payments Adversely Affect CSE Programs?"

Does the CSE Incentive Payment System Reward Good Performance?

According to OCSE, all states received a CSE incentive payment in FY2011. This means that all states attained a certain level of program performance. According to OCSE, for all five performance measures, all states[42] achieved applicable percentage scores that earned them incentives. Moreover, a comparison of FY2002 data to FY2011 data shows that CSE program performance has improved for all five performance measures. The national average for the paternity establishment score increased from 73% (average of both the CSE measure and the statewide measure) in FY2002 to 98% in FY2011; the score for child support order establishment increased from 70% to 81%; the score for current child support collections increased from 58% to 62%; the score for child support arrearage cases increased from 60% to 62%; and the cost-effectiveness score increased from 4.13 to 5.12.

As discussed in the following sections, the design of the CSE incentive payment system raises questions about whether it is too heavily based on child support collections, and whether artificial thresholds adversely affect performance levels in that they unfairly allow states that are performing at significantly higher levels than other states to be given the same score (at the high end of the performance scale and at the low end of the performance scale).

CSE Collections

Ultimately the amount of a state's incentive payment depends on how much the state collects in child support payments. If a state has a small amount of child CSE collections, then even if it has high performance percentages for all five measures, its CSE incentive payment would be small.

Total child support collections for a state may vary for a number of reasons. Some factors that may influence the amount of child support a state collects include the population of the state, the number of single parents in the state, the number of children in the state, the number of unmarried parents in the state, the number of successful paternity determinations, the number of successful child support order establishments, the size of the TANF caseload, the size of the former-TANF caseload, the number of interstate cases, the effectiveness of the state's CSE program, state per capita income, state child poverty rate, and unemployment rate.

---

[42] One jurisdiction, the Virgin Islands, received incentive payments in four rather than five performance areas. The Virgin Islands failed to meet the cost-effectiveness threshold.

Artificial Thresholds Related to Performance Levels

All of the performance measures have a sliding scale so that increased performance earns a higher level of the incentive payment. However, they also all have upper and lower thresholds.[43] This means that above a certain percentage, all percentages are translated into the maximum applicable percentage. By the same policy, all performance percentages that are below a certain threshold percentage are translated into zero (i.e., the state would not be eligible for an incentive payment), unless the program improves sufficiently and quickly.

For performance measures pertaining to the establishment of paternity or the establishment of child support orders, if a state establishes paternity for at least 80% of its caseload or establishes a child support order for at least 80% of its caseload, the state receives a percentage score of 100%. In FY2011, this meant that Illinois, a state that established paternity for 84.95% of the children in the state without legally identified fathers, and Arizona, a state that established paternity for 126.33%[44] of the children in the state without legally identified fathers, both received a paternity establishment percentage score of 100%. (See **Table B-5**.) Thus, states separated by more than 40 percentage points received the same performance ranking—thereby not fully rewarding the performance of the more successful state. With regard to the establishment of child support orders, in FY2011, South Dakota, a state with an order establishment percentage of 93.06%, received the maximum possible percentage score of 100% as did Illinois, a state with a child support order establishment percentage of 80.13% (See **Table B-5**.)

By the same reasoning, the lower threshold of 50% treats states establishing zero paternities and zero child support orders the same as states establishing paternities or child support orders for 49% of their caseload. (In FY2011, no jurisdiction had an applicable percentage score below 50% for either paternity establishment or child support order establishment.)

The upper threshold for the current collections performance measure also is 80% but the lower threshold is 40%. The performance measure for current child support collections is based on the amount of collections (i.e., a dollar measure). In FY2011, one state (Pennsylvania, 83.90%) exceeded the upper threshold and thereby received a score of 100%. The other states had scores that were less than the upper threshold and more than the lower threshold. The lowest percentage attained was 51.11% (Nevada). (See **Table B-5**.)

Likewise, the upper threshold for the arrearage (i.e., past-due) collections performance measure is 80% and the lower threshold is 40%.[45] The performance measure for arrearage child support collections assesses the state's efforts to collect money from noncustodial parents for past-due support (i.e., a case ["person"] measure). In FY2011, one state (Pennslyvania, 83.77%) exceeded the upper threshold and

---

[43] P.L. 104-193 (enacted August 22, 1996), the 1996 welfare reform law directed the HHS Secretary to develop a new revenue-neutral performance-based incentive payment system in consultation with state CSE directors. The federal Office of Child Support Enforcement (OCSE) convened an Incentive Funding Work Group in late 1996 to develop a new incentive payment system. The work group consisted of 26 persons representing state and local CSE programs, HHS regional offices, and the OCSE central office. The work group determined the minimum and maximum standards (i.e., thresholds) for each performance measure based on historic performance by the states and state trends. In general, the upper threshold was based on the view that most states could realistically achieve that level of performance.

[44] States are able to establish paternities for more than 100% of children needing paternity established because the paternity establishment performance measure compares current year data to previous year's data and includes paternity established on behalf of newborns born outside of marriage as well as older children who were born outside of marriage.

[45] States that fail to attain an applicable percentage score of 40% with respect to arrearage collections can still earn an incentive payment if the state improves its performance by at least 5 percentage points over its previous year's score. A financial penalty is not imposed on states that fail to meet specified performance levels with respect to the arrearage collections performance measure.

thereby received a score of 100%. The other states had scores that were less than the upper threshold and more than the lower threshold. The lowest percentage attained was 45.37% (Hawaii). (See **Table B-5.**)

The upper threshold for the cost-effectiveness performance measure is 5.0 and the lower threshold is 2.0. In FY2011, South Dakota had a cost-effectiveness score of 10.41 and Louisiana had a score of 5.05. Even though there was a 5.36 percentage point difference between the two states, the applicable incentive percentage for those two states and the other 27 states with scores of at least 5.0 was 100%. In FY2011, only one jurisdiction (the Virgin Islands, 1.98) was below the lower threshold of 2.0. (See **Table B-5.**)

There have been several criticisms of the CSE performance thresholds,[46] namely that the upper thresholds are too low. Some observers contend that the numerical percentages of the thresholds were established in law almost 15 years ago and that they no longer represent a measure that challenges states. They argue that although you do not want an upper threshold that is unattainable, you do want one that will encourage states to improve their performance. Others note that because the thresholds were somewhat arbitrary to begin with, it is important to adjust them over time in order to challenge states to keep improving in the specified areas. It has also been mentioned that perhaps there should be an adjustment for population size as well as certain social and/or economic factors such as high level of nonmarital births in a state and low employment rates. In contrast, those who support the current performance standards say that it is unfair to raise the bar just because states are doing a good job. They contend that especially during these times of reduced resources, states are doing more with less and should not be penalized by increasing performance thresholds.

Should Incentive Payments Be Based on Additional Performance Indicators?

The establishment and implementation of the current CSE incentive payment system was in part a recognition that a single indicator (i.e., cost-effectiveness) could not effectively evaluate the performance of the CSE program. The current CSE incentive payment system bases incentives on the state's success in achieving a number of goals, in addition to its ability to provide services in a cost-effective manner. Incentive payments are tied to the rates of paternity establishment, child support order establishment, collection of current child support payments, and collection of arrearages (past-due child support payments), as well as the amount of child support collected for each dollar spent (i.e., cost-effectiveness).

Some in the CSE community contend that several other indicators of performance have just as much legitimacy as the five measures that were enacted.[47] They include medical child support, interstate collections, welfare cost avoidance, payment processing performance, and customer service. In contrast, according to a report on the implementation of the CSE incentive payment system, many states indicated that the five measures were adequate and that adding new ones would be premature.[48]

---

[46] Office of Child Support Enforcement, *Report on State Child Support Enforcement Performance Penalties: Recommendations of the State/Federal Penalties Work Group*, July 27, 1998. See also: *Study of the Implementation of the Performance-Based Incentive System—Final Report*, by the Lewin Group (Karen Gardiner, Michael Fishman, and Asaph Glosser) and ECONorthwest (John Tapogna), Prepared for the Office of Child Support Enforcement, 2004. See also: U.S. Government Accountability Office, *Child Support Enforcement: Departures from Long-term Trends in Sources of Collections and Caseloads Reflect Recent Economic Conditions*, GAO-11-196, January 2011.

[47] *Report on State Child Support Enforcement Performance Penalties: Recommendations of the State/Federal Penalties Work Group*, July 27, 1998, p. 7.

[48] *Study of the Implementation of the Performance-Based Incentive System—Final Report*. Prepared for the Office of Child Support Enforcement by the Lewin Group (Karen N. Gardiner, Michael E. Fishman, and Asaph Glosser) and ECONorthwest (John Tapogna), 2004, pp. 18-19.

Medical Child Support

P.L. 105-200 (enacted in 1998) established the revised CSE incentive payment system and also required the HHS Secretary, in consultation with state CSE directors and representatives of children potentially eligible for medical support, to develop a medical support incentive measure based on the state's effectiveness in establishing and enforcing medical child support obligations. The medical support incentive was to be part of the performance-based child support incentive system.[49] The 1998 law required that a report on this new incentive measure be submitted to Congress not later than October 1, 1999. Although a report was submitted (in March 1999), it recommended that the use of a medical support performance measure be postponed.[50]

To date, the CSE program has never had an incentive performance measure for medical child support. Although medical support data is collected by the states, that information is not currently used to compute incentive payments[51] or penalties and, according to OCSE, there are no immediate plans to use it in connection with the incentive payment system. A medical support incentive measure has been put on hold until OCSE provides further guidance.[52] Medical support data currently provided by states are not required to be determined complete and reliable based on an audit by OCSE.

It should also be noted that although incentive payments are additional income for state CSE programs, in that they are required to be reinvested into the CSE program (or a related activity), they are no longer matched with federal dollars.[53] Thus, their impact on the CSE program has been lessened.[54] In addition, beginning January 1, 2014, the Affordable Care Act (ACA, P.L. 111-148) is expected to expand health insurance coverage to millions of individuals through new health insurance exchanges and expansions in Medicaid. Questions remain, however, regarding how the ACA will impact medical child support.[55]

---

[49] U.S. Department of Health and Human Services, Administration for Children and Families, Office of Child Support Enforcement, *21 Million Children's Health: Our Shared Responsibility*, The Medical Child Support Working Group, June 2000.

[50] At the March 2-3, 1999 meeting, the Medical Child Support Working Group reviewed available data on medical support. Only seven states were able to provide data and some of those states had concerns about its validity. Census data was also reviewed and found to be unsatisfactory because it included information beyond the CSE program's caseload and the data could not be segregated by state. The Working Group agreed that a performance standard for medical support enforcement could not be set based on such limited and invalid data. (Source: U.S. Department of Health and Human Services, Report to the Congress on Development of a Medical Support Incentive for the Child Support Enforcement Program, June 23, 1999.)

[51] Under current federal law, states are accountable for providing reliable data on a timely basis or they receive no incentive payments. The data reliability provisions were enacted as part of P.L. 105-200, which established the current incentive payment system. They are in the law to ensure the integrity of the incentive payment system. The federal Office of Child Support Enforcement (OCSE) Office of Audit performs data reliability audits to evaluate the completeness, accuracy, security, and reliability of data reported and produced by state reporting systems. The audits help ensure that incentives under the Child Support Performance and Incentives Act of 1998 (P.L. 105-200) are earned and paid only on the basis of verifiable data and that the incentive payments system is fair and equitable. If an audit determines that a state's data are not complete and reliable for a given performance measure, the state receives zero payments for that measure. If states do not meet the data quality standards, they do not receive incentive payments and are subject to federal financial penalties.

[52] Office of Child Support Enforcement, Action Transmittal, AT-11-10, *Notice of Changes to the OCSE-157 Form Regarding Medical Support*, October 17, 2011.

[53] Before FY2008, the federal government was required to match (at a 66% rate) incentive funds that states reinvested in the CSE program. P.L. 109-171 prohibited federal matching of incentive payments effective October 1, 2007 (i.e., FY2008). P.L. 111-5 temporarily reinstated federal matching of incentive payments for FY2009 and FY2010. There is currently no federal match on incentive payments.

[54] The previous 66% federal matching rate on incentive payments resulted in a near tripling of state CSE funding—in that for every dollar the state reinvested in the CSE program, the federal government matched that investment with about $2. Thereby, under old law, states were able to significantly leverage their investment through the federal financial structure.

[55] More additional information on medical child support, see CRS Report R43020, *Medical Child Support: Background and Current Policy*, by Carmen Solomon-Fears.

Interstate Collections

Many CSE workers contend that the most difficult child support orders to establish and enforce are interstate cases. Although states are required to cooperate in interstate child support enforcement, problems arise due to the autonomy of local courts. Family law has traditionally been under the jurisdiction of state and local governments, and citizens fall under the jurisdiction of the courts where they live. Many child support advocates argue that a child should not be seriously disadvantaged in obtaining child support just because his or her parents do not live in the same state. Despite several federal enforcement tools intended to facilitate the establishment and enforcement of interstate collections, problems still exist. Given that about 33% of all CSE cases involve more than one state, some analysts maintain that a performance indicator that would measure whether states were successfully establishing and enforcing interstate child support cases would significantly improve the overall effectiveness of the CSE program.

Others acknowledge the importance of interstate collections but argue that states are not yet in a position to perform satisfactorily on an interstate performance measure. They acknowledge that although interstate collections increased by 52% over the thirteen-year period FY1998-FY2011, from $1.032 billion in FY1998 to $1.568 billion in FY2011, interstate collections (i.e., child support collections forwarded to other states) comprised 7% of total CSE collections in FY1998 and 6% of total CSE collections in FY2011.

Welfare Cost Avoidance

Unlike other social services programs, the CSE program is intended to transfer private—not public— funds to nonwelfare families enrolled in the program. Thus, the CSE program imposes personal responsibility on noncustodial parents by requiring them to meet their financial obligations to their children, thereby alleviating taxpayers of this responsibility. These child support payments often reduce government spending by providing families with incomes sufficient to make them ineligible for programs such as TANF.

In FY2009, child support payments enabled 217,000 CSE families to end their TANF eligibility. Research has indicated that families go on welfare less often and leave sooner when they receive reliable child support payments. In addition, federal costs for Medicaid, Supplemental Nutrition Assistance Program (SNAP), and other means-tested programs decrease when both parents support their children.[56]

Although it is difficult to determine *how much* money might have been spent on various public assistance programs without the collection of child support payments, some analysts contend that it would be good public policy to add a performance indicator that attempts to measure—or at least estimate—the impact of CSE collections in reducing or eliminating costs in other public benefit/welfare programs.[57] Other analysts argue that adding a performance indicator to measure welfare cost avoidance would only add more complexity to an already complicated incentive payment system.

---

[56] The Effects of Child Support on Welfare Exits and Re-entries, by Chien-Chung Huang, James Kunz, and Irwin Garfinkel. *Journal of Policy Analysis and Management, Vol. 21, No. 4*, p. 557-576 (2002); http://www.lafollette.wisc.edu/Courses/PA882/ Huangm%20et%20al_JPAM.pdf.

[57] Urban Institute, prepared for the Department of Health and Human Services, Administration for Children and Families, Office of Child Support Enforcement, *Child Support Cost Avoidance in 1999, Final Report*, by Laura Wheaton, June 6, 2003, Contract No. 105-00-8303; http://www.acf.dhhs.gov/programs/cse/pubs/2003/reports/cost_avoidance/#N10026.

Payment Processing Performance

Some state policymakers and advocates want to look at an even broader set of factors when evaluating their state CSE program. They maintain that a legitimate purpose of performance standards in some instances is to set expectations. They contend that, because the CSE program has expanded its mission from welfare cost recovery to include promotion of self-sufficiency and personal responsibility and service delivery, it should account for payment processing performance. Such a measure would try to capture whether or not child support payments were accurately accounted, whether families were paid in a timely manner, and whether both custodial and noncustodial parents were satisfied with the state's CSE dispute resolution system.[58]

Should TANF Funds Be Reduced Because of Poor CSE Performance?

Several persons who commented on the federal regulations for implementation of the CSE incentive payment and audit penalty provisions said that incentive payments and financial penalties are at odds with each other because they affect different programs (i.e., CSE and TANF).[59] Incentive payments are given to states from federal CSE funding and penalties are taken from a state's TANF funding.[60]

Historically, Congress has linked the CSE program and the TANF (and old AFDC) program. Currently Section 402(a)(2) of the Social Security Act (Title IV-A which deals with TANF (and used to pertain to the AFDC program)) stipulates that the Governor of a state must certify that it will operate an approved CSE program as a condition of receiving TANF block grant funding. Since the enactment of the CSE program in 1975, there has always been a provision in federal law that linked poor performance (and penalties) or noncompliance in the CSE program with a reduction in Title IV-A funding.

The principle that there are levels of state performance that would merit an incentive payment and there are levels that would warrant a penalty was incorporated into the current CSE incentive payment system. But, the law also provides that, before a penalty is imposed, states with lower performance levels may be able to receive some incentive, provided their program improves sufficiently and quickly.[61] States with poor performance are able to still qualify for an incentive payment if a significant increase over the previous year's performance is achieved in those measures (i.e., 10 percentage points on the paternity establishment performance level, 5 percentage points on the child support order establishment performance level, 5 percentage points on the current support collections performance level, and 5 percentage points on the arrearage collections performance level).

Federal law stipulates that with regard to the three "more important" performance measures, states must achieve certain levels of performance in order to avoid being penalized for poor performance. The three

---

[58] National Conference of State Legislatures. *Issue Brief: Accurately Evaluating State Child Support Program Performance*, by Teresa A. Myers; http://www.ncsl.org/programs/cyf/PerformIB.htm.

[59] *Federal Register, Vol. 64, No. 249.* Office of Child Support Enforcement, Department of Health and Human Services. Child Support Enforcement Program; Incentive Payments, Audit Penalties. Final Rule. December 27, 2000 (p. 50 of 71).

[60] Even in cases in which the amount of the child support payment incentive is larger than the amount of the TANF penalty imposed, a state is required to reinvest its incentive payment in its CSE program, while penalties are assessed from the TANF funding stream. States that acquire a penalty would find that each quarterly TANF payment for the upcoming year would be reduced for a total of the TANF penalty amount. These states would then additionally have to expend an equivalent amount of state funds if they wanted to replace the reduction of federal funds.

[61] Under this alternative improvement formula, the CSE incentive payment can never be more than half (50%) of the maximum incentive possible. The cost-effectiveness performance indicator is the only measure whereby improved performance does not translate into an incentive payment.

performance measures are: paternity establishment, child support order establishment, and collection of current child support payments. A graduated penalty equal to a 1% to 5% reduction in federal TANF block grant funds is assessed against states that fail to meet the CSE performance requirements.[62]

Although there is an interaction between the incentive payment and financial penalty systems, they affect different programs. Thus, even if a state's incentive payment is larger than any penalty assessed against the state, the state cannot easily reconcile the difference because the state is required to reinvest incentive payments back into the CSE program. The state would have to expend other state funds (that are not earmarked for the CSE program) to replace the loss in TANF funding.

An alternative to imposing penalties in the form of reducing TANF funding to a state for the inadequacies of its CSE program would be to reduce funding for the CSE program instead. This could be done by taking the financial penalty out of the state's incentive payment and/or subtracting the penalty from the federal government's 66% matching funds to the state.

Why Aren't the Incentives and Penalties Consistent for the Paternity Establishment Performance Measure?

Unlike the other performance measures, the paternity establishment indicator has two separate standards to which it must adhere. First, the Paternity Establishment Percentage (PEP), must meet a 90% standard (Section 452(g) of the Social Security Act). This means that federal law currently requires that states must establish paternity for at least 90% of the children who need to have their father legally identified in order to substantially comply with the requirements of the CSE program.[63]

If a state does not meet the PEP, it must raise its performance by a specified level of improvement in order to avoid having a financial penalty imposed. The percentage of improvement required varies with a state's performance level. The increase needed to avoid a penalty decreases with higher PEP scores until a state reaches a 90% or higher PEP, at which point the penalty is avoided without an increase in performance. For example, a state with a PEP of less than 40% needs a 6 percentage point increase over the prior year to avoid the penalty. Whereas, a state with a PEP between 75% and 90% needs a 2 percentage point increase over the previous year to avoid the penalty.[64] If the state fails to increase the PEP by the

---

[62] The percentage reduction depends on number of times a state fails to comply with CSE state plan requirements (i.e., at least 1% but not more than 2% for the 1st failure to comply, at least 2% but not more than 3% for the 2nd failure, and at least 3% but not more than 5% for the 3rd and subsequent failures).

[63] The original Paternity Establishment Percentage (PEP) was enacted into law as part of the Family Support Act of 1988 (P.L. 100-485, Section 452(g) of the Social Security Act). The Omnibus Budget Reconciliation Act of 1993 (P.L. 103-66) increased the percentage of children for whom a state must establish paternity (PEP) from 50% to 75%. P.L. 103-66 also imposed financial penalties against states that failed to comply with the mandatory paternity standards. The financial penalty translated into a reduction in federal matching funds for the state's AFDC program. P.L. 104-193, the 1996 welfare reform law, raised the PEP from 75% to 90%.

[64] A state with a paternity establishment percentage at a level between 75% and 90% is required to increase its paternity establishment percentage by two percentage points over the previous year's percentage. A state with a paternity establishment percentage at a level between 50% and 75% is required to increase its paternity establishment percentage by three percentage points over the previous year's percentage. A state with a paternity establishment percentage at a level between 45% and 50% is required to increase its paternity establishment percentage by four percentage points over the previous year's percentage. A state with a paternity establishment percentage at a level between 40% and 45% is required to increase its paternity establishment percentage by five percentage points over the previous year's percentage. A state with a paternity establishment percentage at a level less than 40% is required to increase its paternity establishment percentage by six percentage points over the previous year's percentage.

necessary percentage points after a corrective action period, the state is penalized by a 1%-5% reduction in its federal TANF funding.

Second, in a separate provision (Section 458 of the Social Security Act) the PEP is included as one of the five CSE performance measures. Thus, states can receive incentive payments if their PEP meets certain requirements. The incentive payment provision with respect to the PEP is consistent with the view of the CSE community that only poor performance should be penalized. Thus, under the incentive formula, an incentive is awarded to a state with a PEP of 50% or more. The incentive formula provides that a state that achieves a PEP of 80% or more will receive 100% of the applicable state collection's base for that measure. If a state has a PEP of less than 50%, the state must increase its PEP score by at least 10 percentage points over the previous year's score in order to receive an incentive payment.

From the outset of the performance measure debate (1996-1998), there was a concern about whether states should be subject to penalties and be eligible for incentives at the same time. Some argued that the lack of an incentive payment would make some states doubly penalized by not improving performance. It was decided that states should be eligible for incentive payments based on performance even if they were subject to penalties because their performance had not improved to the extent required to avoid the penalty.[65] The work group that developed the current incentive payment system maintained that the existing statutory PEP standard of 90% was too high and that it conflicted with their premise that only very poor performance should be penalized. Thus, the work group overlaid another provision on top of existing law which provided that a state that had a PEP of 80% or higher would receive 100% of the applicable state collection's base for the paternity establishment performance measure. This new PEP for incentive payment purposes created what many maintain is an inconsistency in CSE law.

According to the National Council of Child Support Directors:

> It is inconsistent to reward a state that achieves a paternity establishment percentage of 80% with maximum child support incentive funding, but impose a penalty against the State's TANF funding if a 2 percentage point increase is not achieved between 80% and 90% performance.[66]

The National Council of Child Support Directors recommended that "the paternity establishment penalty provisions set the upper threshold at 80%, which will then make it consistent and uniform with the existing incentive formula under which a state that has a paternity establishment percentage of 80% or more receives 100% of the weight allowable for that measure."[67] If this recommendation was enacted into law, states would be required to establish paternity for at least 80% of the children who need to have their father legally identified rather than 90% (as required by current law).

Should Incentive Payments Be Based on Individual State Performance Rather Than Aggregate State Performance?

The CSE incentive payment system adds an element of uncertainty to what used to be a somewhat predictable source of income for states. Although in the aggregate, states receive higher incentive payments than under the earlier incentive payment system, these totals are a fixed amount, and individual states have to compete with each other for their share of the capped funds. The capped incentive payment system creates an interactive effect—an increase in incentive payments to one state must be matched by a

---

[65] *Incentive Funding Work Group: Report to the Secretary of Health and Human Services.* January 31, 1997. p. 9.

[66] National Council of Child Support Directors. Position Paper on *Paternity Performance Penalty Revisions*, February 24, 2005.

[67] Ibid.

decrease in payments to other states. Similarly, if one state's performance weakens or the state fails an audit, every other state obtains an increase in incentive payments.

Although CSE incentive payments were constructed to compare a state's program performance to itself rather than a "national average," the fixed amount of aggregate incentive payments forces a state to compete with the other states for its share of the aggregate amount.[68]

Under the current incentive system, whether or not a state receives an incentive payment for good performance and the total amount of the incentive payment depend on four factors: the total amount of money available in a given fiscal year from which to make incentive payments, the state's success in obtaining collections on behalf of its caseload, the state's performance in five areas, and the relative success or failure of other states in making collections and meeting these performance criteria. Because the incentive payments are now capped, some states face a loss of incentive payments even if they improve their performance.

Some analysts argue that each state is unique in terms of its CSE caseload and thereby should only have to make improvements over its own performance in previous years with regard to rewarding of incentive payments.[69] Nevertheless, CSE programs are compared to one another in that there is a capped funding source and it must be shared by all. So even though Texas has a large CSE caseload, shares an international border, and has vast cultural and socioeconomic diversity among its residents, its program is in essence compared to that of a small mid-western state or a wealthy northeastern state in determining its share of CSE incentive dollars.

Others contend that if a state deems that it has not received a sufficient amount of incentive payments and that more CSE funding is necessary, it is the state's prerogative to augment federal funding. They maintain that the federal government is carrying too much of the financial burden of the CSE program. They point out that the federal government matches state funds at a 66% rate and additionally provides states with incentive payments.

Will the Elimination of the Federal Match of Incentive Payments Adversely Affect CSE Programs?

As mentioned earlier, the CSE funding structure requires states to spend state dollars on the program in order to receive federal matching funds. CSE incentive payments in past years[70] had been an important source of those state dollars.

---

[68] As noted earlier, P.L. 105-200 stipulated that the aggregate incentive payment to the states could not exceed the following amounts, i.e., $422 million for FY2000, $429 million for FY2001; $450 million for FY2002; $461 million for FY2003, $454 million for FY2004; $446 million for FY2005; $458 million for FY2006; $471 million for FY2007; and $483 million for FY2008. For years after FY2008, the aggregate incentive payment to the states is to be increased to account for inflation. In FY2009, the incentive payment cap was $504 million. It was also $504 million in FY2010, and it was $513 million in FY2011.

[69] *Study of the Implementation of the Performance-Based Incentive System—Final Report*, by the Lewin Group (Karen Gardiner, Michael Fishman, and Asaph Glosser) and ECONorthwest (John Tapogna), Prepared for the Office of Child Support Enforcement, 2004, p. 23. See also: National Child Support Enforcement Association, Resolution on the Incentive Cap, Adopted by NCSEA Board of Directors on August 11, 2001.

[70] A 2003 study and a 2007 study by the Lewin Group indicated that for the nation as a whole, federal CSE incentive payments represented about 25% of CSE financing for the states. In other words, CSE incentive payments represented about 25% of all funds used to draw down the federal match for the CSE program. (Source: The Lewin Group, *Anticipated Effects of the Deficit Reduction Act Provisions on Child Support Program Financing and Performance Summary of Data Analysis and IV-D Director Calls*, Prepared for the National Council of Child Support Directors by the Lewin Group and ECONorthwest, July 20, 2007, p. 4.. (continued...)

Under previous law, the regular 66% federal match on the incentive payment resulted in a substantial increase in state CSE funding—in that for every dollar the state reinvested in the CSE program, the federal government matched that investment with about $2.[71] Thereby, before FY2008 and in FY2009 and FY2010, states were able to significantly leverage their investment through the federal financial structure. For example, in FY2010, actual incentive payments to states amounted to $504 million; the federal match (at the 66% rate) on the incentive payments amounted to almost twice that figure, $978 million, which translated into the state spending $1.482 billion (based solely on incentive payments) on CSE activities.[72] The elimination of federal reimbursement of CSE incentive payments may result in a significant reduction in CSE financing in the future.

It is generally agreed that state spending/investment in the CSE program significantly impacts program performance. Several past studies indicated that most of the best-performing state CSE programs also had the most generous funding levels.[73] Moreover, "Research has shown that reductions in program expenditures due to funding shortfalls negatively affect program performance particularly in regards to labor-intensive initiatives such as support order establishment, arrears collection initiatives, intensive work with hard-to-serve customers, and empoyer initiatives."[74] The elimination of the federal match of incentive payments is expected to reduce overall CSE program expenditures and correspondingly reduce the rate of growth of child support collections. The OCSE expects that while some states will increase their state contributions to cover some of the lost federal funds, they will not completely make up the shortfall and overall CSE expenditures will be reduced.[75]

According to a 2011 Government Accountability Office (GAO) report:

> Several state officials we interviewed confirmed that they were using the reinstated incentive match funds to sustain program operations and avoid layoffs during tight state budget climates. This is unlike prior years, when incentive match funds might have been used for long-term projects because funding was more predictable. Looking to the future, several of the state officials we interviewed described funding uncertainty surrounding the expiration of the incentive match in fiscal year 2011, as well as

---

(...continued)

Also see U.S. Department of Health and Human Services, *State Financing of Child Support Enforcement Programs: Final Report*, prepared for the Assistant Secretary for Planning and Evaluation and the Office of Child Support Enforcement, prepared by Michael E. Fishman, Kristin Dybdal of the Lewin Group, Inc. and John Tapogna of ECONorthwest, September 3, 2003, p. iii.)

[71] The general CSE federal matching rate is 66%. This means that for every dollar that a state spends on its CSE program, the federal government will reimburse the state 66 cents. So if the state spends $1 on its program, the federal share of that expenditure is 66 cents and the state share of that expenditure is 34 cents. The algebraic formula for this relationship is represented by .66/.34=x/1. Thereby, if the state share of the expenditure is $1, the federal share is $1.94 (i.e., the federal share is 1.94 times the state share), and the total expenditure by the state is $2.94 ($1+$1.94). Similarly, if the state share of expenditures amounted solely to the incentive payment of $471 million (i.e., the statutory cap on the aggregate CSE incentive payment for FY2007), the federal share would amount to 1.94 times that amount, or $914 million, translating into $1.385 billion in total CSE expenditures/funding.

[72] Thus under prior law, the incentive payments to the state could be leveraged by about $3 for every $1 expended. This example is based on incentive payment spending (on CSE activities) only. The 3:1 leveraging did not apply to all state expenditures, it only applied to state expenditures that were based on the incentive payments that were reinvested back into the CSE program.

[73] Center for Law and Social Policy. *You Get What You Pay For: How Federal and State Investment Decisions Affect Child Support Performance*, by Vicki Turetsky. December 1998. See also National Conference of State Legislatures. *Issue Brief: Accurately Evaluating State Child Support Program Performance*, by Teresa A. Myers. http://www.ncsl.org/programs/cyf/PerformIB.htm

[74] U.S. Department of Health and Human Services, Administration for Children and Families, Office of Child Support Enforcement, *Child Support Enforcement Annual Report to Congress FY2010*, April 12, 2013, p. 12.

[75] U.S. Department of Health and Human Services. Administration for Children and Families. *Fiscal Year 2008—Justification of Estimates for Appropriations Committees. Child Support Enforcement*. p. 443-445.

state budget situations. Not knowing whether the incentive match will be extended again or how much their future state CSE appropriations will be has made planning more difficult. Several officials emphasized that even states that maintained overall expenditure levels when the incentive match was eliminated in fiscal year 2008 may not be able to do so again in fiscal year 2011, as many state budget situations have worsened since the economic recession. Some officials also noted that the delivery of services beyond the core mission of the CSE program—such as job skills training and fatherhood initiatives—is particularly uncertain. These officials also told us that, although they believe that these services and partnerships are necessary to continue increasing their collections, particularly from noncustodial parents who are underemployed or have barriers to maintaining employment, these services would be reduced to preserve core services in the event of dramatic budget shortfalls.[76]

Many in the CSE community argue that any reduction in the federal government's financial commitment to the CSE system could negatively affect states' ability to serve families.[77] They contend that a cost shift to the states (during a time when many interests are competing for limited state dollars) could jeopardize the effectiveness of the CSE program and thereby could have a negative impact on the children and families the CSE program is designed to serve.

---

[76] U.S. Government Accountability Office, *Child Support Enforcement: Departures from Long-term Trends in Sources of Collections and Caseloads Reflect Recent Economic Conditions*, GAO-11-196, January 2011, pp. 20-21.

[77] According to the Congressional Budget Office cost estimate of the Deficit Reduction Act of 2005: "If states do not adjust their own spending for the child support program in response to the policies, total funding for the program would fall by 15 percent in 2010. CBO expects that states would instead lessen the effect of the policies on total program spending by increasing state spending. That increased state spending would avoid half of the reduction in total spending that would occur if states were to make no change. CBO estimates that the federal share of administrative costs for child support would fall by about $1.8 billion over the 2008-2010 period and by $5.3 billion over the 2008-2015 period. ... Child support funding is used to establish and enforce child support orders and collect money owed to families. CBO expects that lower spending on the child support program would lead to lower collections." (Source: Congressional Budget Office, Cost Estimate, *S. 1932, Deficit Reduction Act of 2005*, January 27, 2006, p. 59.)

Appendix A. Legislative History of CSE Incentive Payments

Before enactment of the CSE program in 1975, when a state or locality collected child support payments from a noncustodial parent on behalf of a family receiving Aid to Families with Dependent Children (AFDC), the federal government was reimbursed for its share of the cost of AFDC payments to the family.[78] Although local units of government (e.g., counties) often enforced child support obligations, in most states they did not make any financial contributions toward funding AFDC benefit payments. Therefore the localities were not eligible for any share of the "savings" that occurred when child support was collected from a noncustodial parent on behalf of an AFDC family. From the debate on the establishment of a CSE program, Congress concluded that a fiscal sharing in the results of child support collections could be a strong incentive for encouraging the local units of government to improve their CSE activities.[79]

P.L. 90-248, Social Security Amendments of 1967 (January 2, 1968)

Although the formal CSE program was not in existence, P.L. 90-248 provided for the development and implementation of a program under which a state agency would undertake the responsibility for (1) determining the paternity of children receiving AFDC and who were born outside of marriage, and (2) securing financial support from the noncustodial parent for these and other children receiving AFDC, using reciprocal arrangements with other states to obtain and enforce court orders for support. (P.L. 89-97, the Social Security Amendments of 1965 (enacted July 30, 1965), allowed states to use the Federal Medical Assistance Percentage (FMAP) to determine federal-state cost sharing for Title IV-A (i.e., AFDC expenditures), which ranged from a minimum of 50% to a maximum of 83%.) Title IV-A included the child support enforcement provisions indicated above. This meant that if a state collected child support payments on behalf of an AFDC family, the federal government would be reimbursed at the state's FMAP. If the state had an FMAP of 60%, the federal government was reimbursed $60 for every $100 the state collected (from the noncustodial parent) in child support payments for AFDC families.

P.L. 93-647, Enactment of the CSE Program[80] (January 4, 1975)

P.L. 93-647 required that if a child support collection were made by any locality in the state or by the state for another state, that locality or state was to receive a special bonus—incentive payment—based on the amount of any child support collected from a noncustodial parent to reimburse amounts paid out as AFDC. The incentive payment was equal to 25% of the amount of child support collected on behalf of AFDC families for the first 12 months and 10% thereafter. The incentive payment came out of the federal share of the child support recovered (i.e., collected) on behalf AFDC families.[81]

---

[78] The federal share of AFDC benefit expenditures ranged from 50% to 83%, depending on state per capita income.

[79] U.S. Senate. Committee on Finance. *Social Services Amendments of 1974; a report to accompany H.R. 17045.* December 14, 1974. S.Rept. 93-1356. p. 50-51.

[80] The CSE program was enacted as Title IV-D of the Social Security Act.

[81] P.L. 93-647 stipulated that child support payments on behalf of AFDC families were to be paid to the states following an assignment of child support rights by the AFDC client to the state. Because federal dollars were used to finance a portion of the state AFDC benefit payment, states were required to split child support payments collected on behalf of AFDC families with the federal government. The child support collections obtained on behalf of AFDC families are divided between the state and the federal government according to their respective share of total AFDC benefit payments (a small percentage of AFDC collections (continued...)

P.L. 95-30, Tax Reduction and Simplification Act of 1977 (May 23, 1977)

P.L. 95-30 changed the rate at which incentives were paid to states and localities for child support collections used to reimburse AFDC payments. This amendment to Section 458 of the Social Security Act simplified the complex process of computing incentive payments at two different rates by adopting a flat 15% incentive payment rate. The incentive payment was now equal to 15% of child support collections made on behalf of AFDC families. The incentive payment came out of the federal share of the child support recovered (i.e., collected) on behalf AFDC families.

P.L. 97-248, Tax Equity and Fiscal Responsibility Act of 1982 (September 3, 1982)

P.L. 97-248 reduced the incentive payment rate from 15% of child support collections made on behalf of AFDC families to 12% of child support collections made on behalf of AFDC families. The incentive payment came out of the federal share of the child support recovered (i.e., collected) on behalf AFDC families.

P.L. 98-378, Child Support Enforcement Amendments of 1984 (August 16, 1984)

P.L. 98-378 significantly revised incentive payments. Instead of making incentive payments to localities and states that collected child support payments on another state's behalf, the federal government made the incentive payments directly to the states[82] and each state was required to pass incentive payments through to local CSE agencies if those agencies shared in funding the state CSE program. In order to improve cost-effectiveness and encourage states to emphasize child support collections on behalf of both AFDC and non-AFDC families, the incentive payment formula was changed so that states were paid a minimum of 6% of their child support collections in AFDC cases and 6% of their child support collections in non-AFDC cases. Under this approach, there was the potential to earn up to 10% of both AFDC and non-AFDC child support collections depending on the state's cost-effectiveness in running a child support program (i.e., ratio of state collections to the state's cost of operating the CSE program). The federal government paid the incentive payments from its share of retained collections for AFDC families and capped the amount of incentive payments any state could earn on the non-AFDC cases at 115%[83] of the AFDC incentive payment earned. The incentive payments came out of the federal share of the child support recovered (i.e., collected) on behalf AFDC families.

(...continued)

is paid directly to families). As noted above, the federal share of AFDC benefit expenditures ranged from 50% to 83%, depending on state per capita income. The federal share is also called the Federal Medical Assistance Percentage or FMAP.

[82] Before 1984, a state that initiated a successful action to collect child support from another state did not receive an incentive payment. Rather, the state that made the collection received the incentive payment. P.L. 98-378 stipulated that each state involved in an interstate child support collection be credited with the collection for purposes of computing the incentive payment. This "double-counting" was intended to encourage states to pursue interstate child support cases as energetically as they pursued intrastate child support cases.

[83] The total amount of incentives awarded for non-AFDC collections could not exceed the amount of the state's incentive payments for AFDC collections for FY1986 and FY1987. The incentive paid for non-AFDC collections was capped at 105% of the incentive for AFDC collections for FY1988, 110% for FY1989, and 115% for FY1990 and years thereafter.

P.L. 100-485, Family Support Act of 1988 (October 13, 1988)

P.L. 100-485 included a provision that authorized Congress to create a U.S. Commission on Interstate Child Support to make recommendations to Congress on improving the child support program. That Commission's report called for a study of the federal funding formula and changes to an incentive structure that is based on performance. In addition, other national organizations, including the National Conference of State Legislatures, the American Public Welfare Association (now the American Public Human Services Association, APHSA), the National Governors Association, and several national advocacy organizations recommended the adoption of a new performance-based incentive system.[84]

P.L. 104-193, The 1996 Welfare Reform Law (August 22, 1996)

The Personal Responsibility and Work Opportunity Reconciliation Act of 1996 (P.L. 104-193) required the HHS Secretary, in consultation with state CSE program directors, to recommend to Congress a new incentive funding system for state CSE programs based on program performance. P.L. 104-193 required that (1) the new incentive funding system be developed in a revenue-neutral manner; (2) the new system provide additional payments to any state based on that state's performance; and (3) the Secretary report to Congress on the proposed new system by March 1, 1997.

The Incentive Funding Workgroup was formed in October 1996. This group consisted of 15 state and local CSE directors or their representatives and 11 federal staff representatives from HHS. Earlier efforts of this state-federal partnership produced the National Strategic Plan for the CSE program and a set of outcome measures to indicate the program's success in achieving the goals and objectives of the plan. Using the same collaboration and consensus-building approach, state and federal partners recommended a new incentive funding system based on the foundation of the CSE National Strategic Plan.

Over a period of three months, recommendations for the new incentive funding system emerged. State partners consulted with state CSE programs not represented directly on the Workgroup. The final recommendations represented a consensus among state and federal partners on the new incentive funding system. The Secretary fully endorsed the incentive formula recommendations. The Secretary's report made recommendations for a new CSE incentive payment system to the House Committee on Ways and Means and the Senate Committee on Finance.[85]

P.L. 105-200, Child Support Performance and Incentive Act of 1998 (July 16, 1998)

Most of the HHS Secretary's recommendations for a new incentive payment system were included in P.L. 105-200. This law replaced the old incentive payment system to states with a revised revenue-neutral incentive payment system that provides (1) incentive payments based on a percentage of the state's collections; (2) incorporation of five performance measures related to establishment of paternity and child

---

[84] The incentive payment system had been criticized for focusing on only one aspect of the CSE program: cost-effectiveness. It was faulted for not rewarding states for other important aspects of child support enforcement, such as paternity and support order establishment. In addition, because all states received the minimum incentive payment amount of 6% of both AFDC and non-AFDC collections regardless of the state's performance, many analysts claimed that the CSE incentive payment system did not have a real incentive effect.

[85] U.S. Department of Health and Human Services. Administration for Children and Families. Office of Child Support Enforcement. *Child Support Enforcement Incentive Funding.* Report to the House of Representatives Committee on Ways and Means and the Senate Committee on Finance. February 1997.

support orders, collections of current and past-due support payments, and cost-effectiveness; (3) phase-in of the incentive system, with it being fully effective beginning in FY2002; (4) mandatory reinvestment of incentive payments into the CSE program (or an activity that contributes to improving the effectiveness or efficiency of the CSE program); and (5) an incentive payment formula weighted in favor of TANF and former TANF families.

P.L. 105-200 required the HHS Secretary to make incentive payments to the states and stipulated that the aggregate incentive payment to the states could not exceed the following amounts: $422 million for FY2000, $429 million for FY2001, $450 million for FY2002,[86] $461 million for FY2003, $454 million for FY2004, $446 million for FY2005, $458 million for FY2006, $471 million for FY2007, and $483 million for FY2008. For years after FY2008, the aggregate incentive payment to the states is to be increased to account for inflation.

P.L. 109-171, Deficit Reduction Act of 2005 (February 8, 2006)

P.L. 109-171 included a provision that eliminated (effective October 1, 2007, i.e., FY2008) the 66% federal match on CSE incentive payments that states, in compliance with federal law, reinvested back into the CSE program.

P.L. 111-5, the American Recovery and Reinvestment Act of 2009 (February 17, 2009)

P.L. 111-5 temporarily reinstated federal matching of incentive payments for FY2009 and FY2010.

---

[86] Before FY2002, CSE incentive payments were paid out of the federal share of child support collected on behalf of TANF families. Since October 1, 2001 (when the revised incentive payment system was fully phased-in), CSE incentive payments have been paid with federal funds that have been specifically appropriated out of the U.S. Treasury.

Appendix B. Tables

Appendix B includes several detailed state tables. Table B-1 shows that all states received incentive payments in FY2002, FY2005, FY2010, and FY2011 and the amounts they received. Table B-2 displays unaudited incentive performance scores for each of the five performance measures for FY2002. Table B-3 displays unaudited incentive performance scores for each of the five performance measures for FY2005. Table B-4 displays unaudited incentive performance scores for each of the five performance measures for FY2010. Table B-5 displays unaudited incentive performance scores for each of the five performance measures for FY2011.[87]

---

[87] OCSE has not yet published actual CSE incentive payment data by state for FY2012.

Table B-1. Actual Incentive Payments, by State, FY2002, FY2005, FY2010, and FY2011

(arranged by state with the highest incentive payment to state with the lowest incentive payment)

	State	FY2002		State	FY2005		State	FY2010		State	FY2011
1	California	36,814,328	1	California	41,743,556	1	Texas	55,115,303	1	Texas	59,639,748
2	Texas	33,815,354	2	Texas	37,594,823	2	California	37,940,293	2	California	37,894,749
3	Ohio	32,204,888	3	Ohio	28,985,608	3	Florida	29,999,032	3	Florida	33,054,957
4	Pennsylvania	30,284,824	4	New York	26,242,919	4	Ohio	29,151,769	4	New York	28,574,341
5	New York	30,176,739	5	Michigan	26,035,157	5	New York	27,395,346	5	Pennsylvania	26,492,989
6	Michigan	30,128,156	6	Pennsylvania	25,422,058	6	Pennsylvania	25,591,364	6	Michigan	24,466,511
7	Florida	21,261,888	7	Florida	25,263,730	7	Michigan	25,178,161	7	Ohio	22,197,109
8	New Jersey	17,367,328	8	New Jersey	15,974,982	8	New Jersey	17,170,697	8	New Jersey	17,015,753
9	Wisconsin	15,924,085	9	Wisconsin	13,748,475	9	Illinois	13,860,612	9	Illinois	15,775,485
10	Washington	15,204,033	10	North Carolina	13,461,627	10	Wisconsin	13,642,213	10	North Carolina	14,789,831
11	Minnesota	13,555,076	11	Washington	12,719,377	11	Georgia	13,476,091	11	Georgia	13,870,407
12	Georgia	11,999,643	12	Minnesota	12,135,231	12	Washington	12,605,105	12	Wisconsin	13,535,312
13	North Carolina	11,741,877	13	Georgia	10,808,188	13	Missouri	12,250,352	13	Washington	12,617,216
14	Virginia	11,212,586	14	Virginia	10,237,234	14	Indiana	12,201,979	14	Missouri	12,098,575
15	Massachusetts	9,717,960	15	Missouri	10,204,439	15	Minnesota	12,093,695	15	Minnesota	11,907,544
16	Maryland	8,749,496	16	Massachusetts	8,898,038	16	Virginia	11,496,244	16	Virginia	11,633,569
17	Missouri	8,496,830	17	Illinois	8,650,633	17	North Carolina	11,190,271	17	Indiana	11,560,438
18	Kentucky	8,088,515	18	Indiana	8,385,495	18	Massachusetts	10,190,207	18	Massachusetts	10,647,319
19	Iowa	7,126,528	19	Tennessee	7,837,795	19	Tennessee	10,122,576	19	Tennessee	10,314,981
20	Tennessee	6,811,758	20	Maryland	7,303,489	20	Kentucky	7,967,078	20	Louisiana	8,029,653
21	Oregon	6,541,362	21	Iowa	6,917,274	21	Louisiana	7,578,061	21	Kentucky	7,836,843
22	Illinois	6,183,369	22	Louisiana	6,213,377	22	Iowa	7,482,967	22	Iowa	7,375,772
23	Indiana	5,564,581	23	Oregon	5,600,727	23	Maryland	7,169,234	23	Maryland	7,268,619
24	Connecticut	5,491,503	24	Arizona	5,423,112	24	Arizona	6,693,262	24	Oklahoma	6,433,082

	State	FY2002		State	FY2005		State	FY2010		State	FY2011
25	Colorado	5,356,965	25	Kentucky	5,208,111	25	Oregon	6,173,524	25	Arizona	6,422,506
26	Arizona	5,206,147	26	Connecticut	4,865,914	26	Oklahoma	5,896,756	26	Oregon	6,238,714
27	Louisiana	4,389,087	27	Colorado	4,750,251	27	Colorado	5,300,432	27	Colorado	5,246,427
28	West Virginia	4,058,389	28	Alabama	4,020,646	28	Connecticut	5,166,296	28	Connecticut	5,058,826
29	South Carolina	3,899,715	29	West Virginia	3,879,643	29	West Virginia	4,702,120	29	Arkansas	4,723,619
30	Arkansas	3,217,437	30	Oklahoma	3,643,878	30	Arkansas	4,588,159	30	Alabama	4,612,658
31	Puerto Rico	3,201,676	31	Nebraska	3,475,303	31	South Carolina	4,543,448	31	Nebraska	4,605,084
32	Utah	3,101,832	32	South Carolina	3,321,883	32	Alabama	4,486,109	32	South Carolina	4,550,967
33	Nebraska	3,056,992	33	Kansas	3,289,970	33	Nebraska	4,380,112	33	Puerto Rico	4,341,887
34	Alabama	2,900,775	34	Utah	3,288,628	34	Puerto Rico	4,360,872	34	Mississippi	4,130,182
35	Oklahoma	2,899,609	35	Puerto Rico	3,268,672	35	Kansas	3,946,123	35	West Virginia	4,098,556
36	Kansas	2,873,656	36	Mississippi	3,222,870	36	Mississippi	3,879,458	36	Kansas	3,990,204
37	Maine	2,596,197	37	Arkansas	2,490,610	37	Utah	3,580,240	37	Utah	3,863,279
38	Mississippi	2,526,611	38	Idaho	2,389,857	38	Idaho	2,827,522	38	Nevada	3,122,406
39	Alaska	1,679,107	39	Maine	2,167,195	39	Nevada	2,806,180	39	Idaho	2,791,858
40	South Dakota	1,656,493	40	Nevada	1,826,744	40	Maine	2,063,954	40	North Dakota	2,027,445
41	Idaho	1,650,232	41	Alaska	1,809,329	41	North Dakota	1,973,912	41	Maine	2,013,957
42	New Hampshire	1,438,353	42	New Hampshire	1,650,128	42	South Dakota	1,815,004	42	New Mexico	1,996,326
43	Montana	1,202,605	43	North Dakota	1,560,854	43	New Mexico	1,808,304	43	South Dakota	1,917,362
44	Wyoming	1,201,957	44	South Dakota	1,466,513	44	Alaska	1,778,401	44	Alaska	1,827,200
45	North Dakota	1,192,916	45	Hawaii	1,431,973	45	New Hampshire	1,733,474	45	New Hampshire	1,736,226
46	Vermont	1,127,161	46	Rhode Island	1,211,250	46	Hawaii	1,625,717	46	Hawaii	1,664,091
47	Delaware	1,034,185	47	Wyoming	1,163,702	47	Wyoming	1,286,050	47	Wyoming	1,311,261
48	Rhode Island	1,016,821	48	New Mexico	1,055,389	48	Delaware	1,262,780	48	Rhode Island	1,260,809
49	Hawaii	973,201	49	Montana	1,028,469	49	Rhode Island	1,204,315	49	Montana	1,194,604
50	Nevada	857,000	50	Vermont	977,267	50	Montana	1,131,812	50	Delaware	1,169,480

Child Support Enforcement Program Incentive Payments: Background and Policy Issues

	State	FY2002		State	FY2005		State	FY2010		State	FY2011
51	New Mexico	554,604	51	Delaware	900,305	51	Vermont	915,231	51	District of Columbia	912,555
52	District of Columbia	502,393	52	District of Columbia	598,507	52	District of Columbia	902,209	52	Vermont	891,151
53	Guam	101,209	53	Guam	119,823	53	Guam	192,683	53	Guam	171,983
54	Virgin Islands	63,968	54	Virgin Islands	108,972	54	Virgin Islands	106,891	54	Virgin Islands	77,575
	Total	**$450,000,000**		**Total**	**$446,000,000**		**Total**	**$504,000,000**		**Total**	**$513,000,000**

Source: Table prepared by the Congressional Research Service based on data from the Office of Child Support Enforcement, Department of Health and Human Services.

Note: The table shows the rank order of each state from state with the highest incentive payment (ranked 1) to the state with the lowest incentive payment (ranked 54). The four jurisdictions of the District of Columbia, Guam, Puerto Rico, and the Virgin Islands are included in the state totals.

Table B-2. Unaudited Child Support Enforcement Incentive Performance Scores, FY2002

(arranged by highest performing state to lowest performing state)

Paternity Establishment Percentage		Cases with Orders Percentage		Current Collections Percentage		Arrearage Cases Percentage		Cost-Effectiveness Score	
State		State		State		State		State	
Guam	452.87a	South Dakota	92.03	Pennsylvania	74.70	New Hampshire	71.58	Indiana	$7.80
Idaho	130.75	Washington	91.00	Minnesota	72.96	Pennsylvania	70.68	South Dakota	7.59
Montana	113.07	Iowa	87.79	Wisconsin	72.68	Vermont	70.64	Mississippi	7.12
Texas	108.43	Maine	87.17	North Dakota	71.55	South Dakota	68.59	Pennsylvania	6.85
California	107.94	Vermont	85.80	South Dakota	67.70	Washington	68.33	Hawaii	6.53
New Hampshire	106.74	Utah	85.11	Ohio	66.77	Delaware	67.83	Virginia	6.34
South Dakota	106.46	North Dakota	84.76	Nebraska	66.49	Ohio	67.46	Puerto Rico	6.27
Pennsylvania	106.01	Colorado	83.46	Vermont	66.34	Alaska	67.39	Wisconsin	6.11
Ohio	103.38	Montana	83.10	New Hampshire	65.51	North Dakota	66.12	South Carolina	5.87
Colorado	102.85	Pennsylvania	82.97	New York	65.12	Colorado	66.10	Oregon	5.85
Washington	100.88	Alaska	82.90	New Jersey	65.00	Utah	66.04	Massachusetts	5.77
Wyoming	97.78	Wyoming	82.75	Washington	63.98	Minnesota	65.07	Iowa	5.63
Illinois	97.06	New Hampshire	82.02	West Virginia	62.33	Texas	64.45	Texas	5.41
Maryland	96.67	Virginia	80.20	Maryland	62.02	Maryland	64.29	Idaho	5.29
Wisconsin	94.50	Wisconsin	78.99	North Carolina	61.26	Montana	63.72	Wyoming	5.00
Oregon	94.40	Missouri	78.93	Rhode Island	61.11	Iowa	63.34	Washington	4.95
Vermont	94.08	New Jersey	78.90	Delaware	60.74	Florida	62.83	Louisiana	4.87
Maine	93.56	Idaho	78.64	Oregon	60.41	Nevada	62.03	West Virginia	4.87
Michigan	92.04	Arkansas	78.53	Wyoming	60.05	Nebraska	61.66	New Jersey	4.83
West Virginia	90.49	Minnesota	78.04	Texas	59.93	Wyoming	61.57	Ohio	4.81
Utah	90.27	Michigan	76.22	Massachusetts	59.68	Maine	61.25	Kentucky	4.71
Virginia	90.14	Nebraska	76.04	Michigan	59.36	New Jersey	61.18	North Dakota	4.71

State	Paternity Establishment Percentage	State	Cases with Orders Percentage	State	Current Collections Percentage	State	Arrearage Cases Percentage	State	Cost-Effectiveness Score
Alaska	89.64	California	75.32	Iowa	59.10	Wisconsin	61.07	Missouri	4.63
Puerto Rico	88.17	West Virginia	74.90	Virginia	58.97	Oregon	61.04	Michigan	4.59
New York	87.77	North Carolina	73.15	Utah	58.60	Kansas	61.03	Rhode Island	4.52
Iowa	87.57	New York	73.05	Montana	58.50	Georgia	60.78	Tennessee	4.50
North Dakota	87.40	Ohio	71.38	Maine	57.76	Michigan	60.78	Alaska	4.49
Arkansas	85.88	Massachusetts	71.17	Louisiana	56.44	Louisiana	60.63	New York	4.49
Connecticut	85.06	Indiana	70.59	Florida	56.40	New York	60.43	North Carolina	4.43
North Carolina	84.41	Delaware	70.34	Idaho	55.43	New Mexico	60.33	New Hampshire	4.37
Georgia	83.25	Kentucky	70.04	Kansas	55.06	North Carolina	60.32	Maine	4.28
Kentucky	82.54	Oklahoma	69.69	Connecticut	55.04	Idaho	60.11	Arizona	4.25
Massachusetts	82.45	Texas	69.00	Colorado	54.97	Mississippi	59.84	Georgia	4.24
Minnesota	82.06	Maryland	68.65	Alaska	53.84	Massachusetts	58.32	Maryland	4.19
South Carolina	81.44	Georgia	68.16	Kentucky	52.80	Rhode Island	58.19	Montana	4.10
Hawaii	81.41	Louisiana	67.36	Hawaii	51.13	West Virginia	57.53	Minnesota	4.05
New Jersey	81.37	Arizona	66.99	Missouri	50.74	Oklahoma	56.78	Florida	4.03
Nebraska	81.03	Oregon	66.91	Tennessee	50.44	Virginia	56.37	Vermont	3.93
Oklahoma	80.69	South Carolina	66.71	Arkansas	50.32	Arkansas	55.53	Utah	3.89
Florida	80.10	Alabama	66.22	Georgia	49.73	California	54.92	Connecticut	3.76
Missouri	79.74	Florida	65.23	Mississippi	49.55	Tennessee	54.54	Colorado	3.66
Delaware	77.21	Connecticut	64.34	South Carolina	49.51	Connecticut	53.13	Delaware	3.66
Tennessee	76.94	Puerto Rico	63.91	Puerto Rico	48.67	Indiana	52.58	Alabama	3.64
Louisiana	76.83	Kansas	63.76	Indiana	48.52	Illinois	52.30	Nebraska	2.87
Dist. of Columbia	75.23	Nevada	60.35	Dist. of Columbia	47.96	South Carolina	51.84	Nevada	2.87
Kansas	74.75	Hawaii	59.22	Alabama	47.77	Puerto Rico	50.84	Illinois	2.80
Mississippi	69.82	Tennessee	56.55	Virgin Islands	47.02	Arizona	50.63	Oklahoma	2.80

State	Paternity Establishment Percentage	State	Cases with Orders Percentage	State	Current Collections Percentage	State	Arrearage Cases Percentage	State	Cost-Effectiveness Score
Rhode Island	68.85	Rhode Island	51.24	Nevada	46.99	Missouri	50.00	Dist. of Columbia	2.69
Nevada	67.89	Guam	50.17	New Mexico	46.75	Kentucky	49.97	Arkansas	2.66
Alabama	65.39	Mississippi	49.84	Oklahoma	46.46	Virgin Islands	48.69	Kansas	2.61
New Mexico	57.61	New Mexico	47.51	Arizona	44.48	Alabama	47.95	California	1.91
Virgin Islands	52.94	Illinois	40.82	Guam	43.16	Guam	37.08	Guam	1.64
Arizona	51.02	Virgin Islands	38.07	California	42.40	Hawaii	36.87	Virgin Islands	1.58
Indiana	50.83	Dist. of Columbia	29.66	Illinois	39.11	Dist. of Columbia	30.21	New Mexico	$1.46

Source: Table prepared by the Congressional Research Service based on data from the Office of Child Support Enforcement, Department of Health and Human Services.

Note: The paternity establishment percentage can be greater than 100% because states can take credit for paternities established for children of any age and compare that number established to the number of births outside of marriage for a single year.

a. Because of conflicting information and data in other reports Guam's PEP score of 452.87 was excluded from this report's analysis.

Table B-3. Unaudited Child Support Enforcement Incentive Performance Scores, FY2005

(arranged by highest performing state to lowest performing state)

State	Paternity Establishment Percentage	State	Cases with Orders Percentage	State	Current Collections Percentage	State	Arrearage Cases Percentage	State	Cost Effectiveness Score
Oklahoma	112.42	South Dakota	96.00	Pennsylvania	74.72	Pennsylvania	73.50	Indiana	$8.53
Maine	111.02	Alaska	92.41	North Dakota	72.70	New Hampshire	71.97	Mississippi	8.53
Texas	107.95	Washington	89.57	Minnesota	69.31	Vermont	71.01	South Dakota	7.76
California	106.54	Wyoming	89.38	South Dakota	69.04	North Dakota	69.69	South Carolina	7.07
Montana	105.43	Maine	89.10	Wisconsin	69.01	South Dakota	69.52	Texas	6.81
Alaska	104.79	Montana	88.12	Ohio	68.98	Wyoming	67.76	Michigan	6.70
Puerto Rico	104.40	Vermont	88.02	Nebraska	67.84	Utah	67.57	Virginia	6.52
Ohio	104.13	North Dakota	86.75	Vermont	66.98	Alaska	67.46	Rhode Island	6.45
South Dakota	103.56	Colorado	85.38	New Jersey	65.27	Florida	66.71	Pennsylvania	6.39
North Dakota	102.88	Iowa	85.35	New York	65.13	Ohio	66.54	Wyoming	6.25
New Hampshire	102.53	Utah	85.25	Iowa	64.74	Washington	66.11	North Dakota	6.03
New Jersey	100.45	Pennsylvania	84.71	New Hampshire	64.63	Minnesota	66.08	Puerto Rico	6.01
Wisconsin	100.23	Virginia	84.68	North Carolina	64.52	Iowa	65.70	Kentucky	5.95
Florida	99.90	Wisconsin	83.55	Massachusetts	63.79	Colorado	65.65	Massachusetts	5.93
Vermont	98.82	West Virginia	83.54	West Virginia	63.69	Texas	65.23	Oregon	5.93
Pennsylvania	98.73	Arkansas	82.41	Wyoming	63.67	Nebraska	64.96	Iowa	5.80
Hawaii	98.09	Texas	82.23	Washington	63.31	Wisconsin	64.19	Ohio	5.66
North Carolina	96.37	Minnesota	82.12	Maryland	63.08	Montana	64.14	Idaho	5.58
Minnesota	96.09	Missouri	81.63	Utah	61.39	Maryland	63.92	Tennessee	5.44
Washington	95.16	New Hampshire	81.15	Virginia	60.91	Delaware	63.71	Missouri	5.41
Iowa	94.76	North Carolina	80.88	Montana	60.68	New Jersey	63.20	Wisconsin	5.41
Idaho	93.97	New Jersey	80.72	Rhode Island	60.63	West Virginia	62.88	Georgia	5.20
Kentucky	92.53	California	80.28	Michigan	60.52	Kansas	62.59	North Carolina	5.10

State	Paternity Establishment Percentage	State	Cases with Orders Percentage	State	Current Collections Percentage	State	Arrearage Cases Percentage	State	Cost Effectiveness Score
Missouri	92.52	New York	80.03	Texas	60.51	North Carolina	62.16	West Virginia	4.90
Colorado	92.36	Idaho	78.58	Delaware	60.41	New Mexico	61.32	Maryland	4.88
Illinois	92.19	Nebraska	77.72	Maine	60.30	Arkansas	60.87	Florida	4.80
Oregon	91.71	Kentucky	77.51	Oregon	60.09	Oregon	60.72	New York	4.79
Massachusetts	91.22	Maryland	74.65	Colorado	57.69	Mississippi	60.46	New Hampshire	4.75
Kansas	91.19	Michigan	74.50	Arkansas	57.09	Tennessee	60.05	New Jersey	4.74
Arkansas	90.57	Georgia	74.47	Florida	56.72	Georgia	59.16	Washington	4.74
Maryland	90.57	Kansas	74.41	Idaho	55.81	New York	59.02	Arizona	4.73
New York	90.33	Alabama	73.93	Virgin Islands	55.66	Rhode Island	58.03	Louisiana	4.71
Virginia	89.34	Arizona	73.91	Louisiana	55.45	Indiana	58.01	Alaska	4.54
Connecticut	87.87	Delaware	73.83	Tennessee	55.43	Massachusetts	57.86	Hawaii	4.39
West Virginia	87.65	Massachusetts	73.60	Connecticut	55.38	Virginia	57.76	Maine	4.27
Michigan	86.46	Ohio	72.69	Kentucky	55.31	Louisiana	57.64	Alabama	4.26
South Carolina	84.67	Florida	72.18	Hawaii	55.30	California	56.03	Minnesota	4.22
Georgia	83.69	Louisiana	71.99	Puerto Rico	55.28	Connecticut	55.51	Utah	4.03
Utah	83.47	South Carolina	71.23	Alaska	54.96	Oklahoma	55.18	Montana	4.02
Wyoming	82.90	Connecticut	69.52	Missouri	54.69	Idaho	54.66	Vermont	3.91
Nebraska	82.49	Indiana	69.39	Kansas	54.52	South Carolina	53.80	Oklahoma	3.79
Indiana	82.28	Oklahoma	69.09	Mississippi	53.47	Kentucky	53.44	Arkansas	3.68
Louisiana	81.93	Oregon	67.41	Illinois	53.29	Michigan	53.18	Colorado	3.68
Alabama	81.89	Puerto Rico	66.37	Dist. of Columbia	52.89	Maine	52.96	Connecticut	3.68
Arizona	81.11	Tennessee	64.84	Indiana	52.82	Puerto Rico	52.55	Illinois	3.68
Tennessee	80.48	Nevada	62.41	Georgia	52.56	Missouri	52.10	Nebraska	3.57
Virgin Islands	79.56	Guam	60.18	Alabama	51.74	Arizona	51.37	Kansas	3.39
Guam	79.27	New Mexico	59.83	Oklahoma	50.11	Guam	50.33	Delaware	3.10

Child Support Enforcement Program Incentive Payments: Background and Policy Issues

State	Paternity Establishment Percentage	State	Cases with Orders Percentage	State	Current Collections Percentage	State	Arrearage Cases Percentage	State	Cost Effectiveness Score
Delaware	79.14	Illinois	59.35	New Mexico	50.00	Alabama	49.96	Nevada	2.98
Mississippi	77.80	Hawaii	58.30	California	49.27	Nevada	49.60	Dist. of Columbia	2.45
Rhode Island	77.02	Rhode Island	57.18	South Carolina	47.41	Virgin Islands	47.78	California	2.15
Dist. of Columbia	74.81	Virgin Islands	55.41	Guam	47.33	Illinois	45.91	Guam	2.11
Nevada	66.30	Mississippi	53.63	Nevada	45.68	Dist. of Columbia	43.68	Virgin Islands	2.11
New Mexico	54.05	Dist. of Columbia	39.60	Arizona	44.36	Hawaii	41.36	New Mexico	$2.10

Source: Table prepared by the Congressional Research Service based on data from the Office of Child Support Enforcement, Department of Health and Human Services.

Note: The paternity establishment percentage can be greater than 100% because states can take credit for paternities established for children of any age and compare that number established to the number of births outside of marriage for a single year.

Table B-4. Unaudited Child Support Enforcement Incentive Performance Scores, FY2010

(arranged by highest performing state to lowest performing state)

State	Paternity Establishment Percentage	State	Cases with Orders Percentage	State	Current Collections Percentage	State	Arrearage Cases Percentage	State	Cost Effectiveness Score
Arizona	118.29	South Dakota	92.38	Pennsylvania	83.24	Pennsylvania	83.14	Wyoming	$12.54
Montana	108.31	Wyoming	91.00	North Dakota	74.21	West Virginia	71.40	South Dakota	11.34
North Dakota	108.14	Vermont	90.05	Wisconsin	70.58	Minnesota	70.02	Puerto Rico	10.23
New Hampshire	107.10	Pennsylvania	89.90	Iowa	69.75	Colorado	69.65	Texas	8.80
Oklahoma	106.99	North Dakota	89.78	Minnesota	69.63	Vermont	69.18	Indiana	7.43
Maine	105.11	Washington	89.47	Nebraska	68.99	Wyoming	68.91	Kentucky	6.84
West Virginia	104.91	Alaska	89.44	South Dakota	68.88	Iowa	68.82	Virginia	6.83
South Dakota	104.37	Kentucky	88.69	Massachusetts	67.89	New Hampshire	68.82	Missouri	6.71
Vermont	104.03	Maine	88.35	Vermont	67.62	North Dakota	68.70	Tennessee	6.68
California	102.57	Colorado	88.09	New York	66.95	Georgia	68.17	Georgia	6.58
Indiana	102.16	Montana	87.61	Ohio	66.62	Nebraska	68.05	Michigan	6.55
Washington	101.44	Utah	87.56	Washington	65.79	New Mexico	67.11	Ohio	6.54
Minnesota	100.39	Missouri	86.45	North Carolina	65.21	South Dakota	66.76	Idaho	6.03
Nevada	100.30	Virginia	86.39	Wyoming	65.14	Arkansas	66.43	Iowa	6.02
Wisconsin	100.17	West Virginia	86.21	New Jersey	65.05	Alaska	65.89	Arizona	5.84
North Carolina	99.80	Wisconsin	85.33	Maryland	64.46	Montana	65.86	Wisconsin	5.81
Pennsylvania	98.21	Minnesota	85.27	West Virginia	64.20	Utah	64.89	Mississippi	5.74
Puerto Rico	97.67	Iowa	85.06	Texas	63.44	Texas	64.51	Pennsylvania	5.68
Colorado	97.37	New Hampshire	85.05	Colorado	62.70	Indiana	64.14	North Dakota	5.61
Utah	97.22	Arkansas	84.73	Michigan	62.45	Ohio	64.01	North Carolina	5.36
Arkansas	97.22	Georgia	84.33	Arkansas	62.31	North Carolina	63.67	Oregon	5.29
New Jersey	95.64	Nebraska	83.88	Virginia	61.96	Guam	63.57	Florida	5.12
Virginia	95.51	Arizona	83.79	Hawaii	61.58	Kansas	63.30	West Virginia	5.03

State	Paternity Establishment Percentage	State	Cases with Orders Percentage	State	Current Collections Percentage	State	Arrearage Cases Percentage	State	Cost Effectiveness Score
Hawaii	95.19	Maryland	82.82	Guam	60.99	Washington	62.87	Massachusetts	4.87
Nebraska	94.82	California	82.55	Utah	60.97	New Jersey	62.40	Nebraska	4.84
Alabama	94.76	Idaho	82.43	New Hampshire	60.94	Wisconsin	62.09	South Carolina	4.80
Texas	94.69	Alabama	82.36	Montana	60.80	Maryland	61.57	Louisiana	4.69
Kentucky	94.48	Texas	82.06	Georgia	60.67	Oklahoma	61.35	New York	4.69
Michigan	94.25	Massachusetts	81.90	Maine	60.41	Illinois	61.33	Illinois	4.56
Connecticut	93.91	North Carolina	81.18	Rhode Island	60.35	Massachusetts	60.70	Washington	4.43
Ohio	93.90	New Jersey	80.95	Virginia	59.98	Virginia	60.48	New Jersey	4.37
New Mexico	93.13	Kansas	80.31	California	59.96	Hawaii	60.29	Hawaii	4.36
Rhode Island	92.90	New York	80.05	Florida	59.29	Montana	59.93	Montana	4.31
Massachusetts	92.89	Michigan	79.16	Mississippi	58.48	Alabama	59.65	Alabama	4.28
Alaska	92.68	Louisiana	78.47	Oregon	58.28	Utah	59.30	Utah	4.21
Iowa	92.57	Ohio	77.70	Connecticut	58.09	Colorado	59.26	Colorado	4.19
Georgia	92.52	Illinois	77.66	New York	58.06	New Hampshire	59.15	New Hampshire	4.18
Oregon	92.19	Puerto Rico	77.10	Kentucky	57.92	Alaska	58.96	Alaska	4.11
Florida	91.46	Guam	77.05	Missouri	57.85	Oklahoma	58.25	Oklahoma	4.03
Illinois	90.77	Nevada	76.48	Maine	56.70	Maine	58.03	Maine	3.80
Missouri	90.65	Indiana	75.99	Delaware	56.65	Connecticut	58.01	Connecticut	3.71
Idaho	90.64	Oregon	74.71	Tennessee	56.63	Minnesota	57.45	Minnesota	3.70
New York	90.60	Oklahoma	74.62	Louisiana	55.98	Arkansas	57.31	Arkansas	3.68
Kansas	90.51	Florida	73.50	Idaho	55.96	Maryland	57.25	Maryland	3.58
South Carolina	90.46	Connecticut	73.22	Michigan	55.30	Kansas	57.10	Kansas	3.41
Tennessee	90.28	Hawaii	69.29	Nevada	55.26	Vermont	56.80	Vermont	3.37
Louisiana	90.27	Tennessee	68.88	New Mexico	54.97	Rhode Island	56.05	Rhode Island	3.31
Virgin Islands	90.26	New Mexico	68.34	Oklahoma	54.74	Alabama	55.42	Delaware	3.22

State	Paternity Establish-ment Percentage	State	Cases with Orders Percentage	State	Current Collections Percentage	State	Arrearage Cases Percentage	State	Cost Effective-ness Score
Maryland	89.47	Delaware	67.09	Florida	52.16	Arizona	54.14	Nevada	2.92
Guam	88.60	South Carolina	66.75	South Carolina	51.89	South Carolina	54.01	Guam	2.66
Dist. of Columbia	88.35	Rhode Island	64.96	Tennessee	51.87	Puerto Rico	53.29	New Mexico	2.54
Wyoming	84.99	Dist. of Columbia	64.76	Arizona	50.82	Virgin Islands	51.39	California	2.38
Mississippi	82.09	Virgin Islands	63.03	Alabama	50.20	Dist. of Columbia	49.71	Dist. of Columbia	2.10
Delaware	81.26	Mississippi	56.87	Nevada	49.10	Hawaii	45.61	Virgin Islands	$1.42

Source: Table prepared by the Congressional Research Service based on data from the Office of Child Support Enforcement, Department of Health and Human Services.

Note: The paternity establishment percentage can be greater than 100% because states can take credit for paternities established for children of any age and compare that number established to the number of births outside of marriage for a single year.

Table B-5. Unaudited Child Support Enforcement Incentive Performance Scores, FY2011

(arranged by highest performing state to lowest performing state)

State	Paternity Establishment Percentage	State	Cases with Orders Percentage	State	Current Collections Percentage	State	Arrearage Cases Percentage	State	Cost Effectiveness Score
Arizona	126.33	South Dakota	93.06	Pennsylvania	83.90	Pennsylvania	83.77	South Dakota	$10.41
Oklahoma	112.76	Wyoming	92.50	North Dakota	74.57	Wyoming	72.18	Mississippi	9.79
North Dakota	109.50	Alaska	91.76	Iowa	71.66	Minnesota	70.53	Massachusetts	9.45
Nevada	109.30	North Dakota	89.84	Wisconsin	70.59	Iowa	70.27	Texas	9.29
South Dakota	108.22	Washington	89.77	Minnesota	70.48	Vermont	69.96	Puerto Rico	8.86
Montana	107.05	Maine	89.74	Nebraska	69.75	Colorado	69.88	Missouri	7.46
California	106.95	Vermont	89.65	Colorado	69.00	Nebraska	69.06	Tennessee	7.31
New Hampshire	105.61	Pennsylvania	89.39	Nebraska	68.23	North Dakota	69.00	Georgia	7.02
Indiana	104.09	Kentucky	89.03	North Dakota	68.03	New Mexico	67.39	Virginia	6.99
Vermont	103.84	Montana	88.77	New Mexico	66.63	Georgia	66.75	Idaho	6.94
Utah	103.80	Utah	88.04	Georgia	66.61	Idaho	66.33	Ohio	6.77
Colorado	103.02	West Virginia	87.88	South Dakota	66.43	Ohio	66.31	Wisconsin	6.44
West Virginia	102.81	Iowa	87.26	Alaska	65.68	Wisconsin	66.14	North Dakota	6.32
Washington	101.60	Virginia	87.22	Arkansas	65.26	North Dakota	65.94	Iowa	6.24
Wisconsin	101.38	North Carolina	86.46	Montana	64.83	Iowa	65.19	Michigan	6.18
Minnesota	101.37	Colorado	86.43	New Hampshire	64.70	Michigan	65.07	Arizona	6.03
Alaska	101.28	New Hampshire	86.02	Texas	64.66	Arizona	64.81	Kentucky	5.99
Maine	100.53	Minnesota	85.92	Guam	64.64	Kentucky	64.69	Hawaii	5.95
New Jersey	99.92	Idaho	85.91	Indiana	63.39	Hawaii	64.53	Pennsylvania	5.80
North Carolina	99.74	Missouri	85.81	North Carolina	63.32	Pennsylvania	64.15	Nebraska	5.78
Hawaii	99.47	California	85.30	Utah	62.81	Nebraska	64.14	Utah	5.59
Georgia	98.80	Arkansas	85.09	Ohio	62.52	Utah	63.47	North Carolina	5.55
Arkansas	98.11	Arizona	84.78	Wisconsin	62.31	North Carolina	62.95	New York	5.47

State	Paternity Establishment Percentage	State	Cases with Orders Percentage	State	Current Collections Percentage	State	Arrearage Cases Percentage	State	Cost Effectiveness Score
Iowa	97.80	New Hampshire	84.63	New Jersey	62.05	Florida	62.37	Florida	5.44
Texas	97.60	Michigan	83.44	Oklahoma	62.00	Oregon	61.64	Oregon	5.41
Puerto Rico	97.39	Arkansas	83.31	California	61.58	Indiana	61.58	Indiana	5.35
Pennsylvania	97.32	Georgia	82.90	Maryland	60.79	Wyoming	61.57	Wyoming	5.30
Kentucky	95.93	Utah	82.90	Washington	60.03	Montana	61.45	Montana	5.13
New Mexico	94.80	Dist. of Columbia	82.56	Virginia	59.97	Louisiana	61.38	Louisiana	5.05
Alabama	94.63	Rhode Island	82.21	Illinois	59.93	West Virginia	61.19	West Virginia	4.73
Wyoming	94.50	Idaho	82.01	West Virginia	59.90	Illinois	61.00	Illinois	4.72
Connecticut	94.47	Delaware	80.96	Florida	59.79	Washington	60.76	Washington	4.68
Florida	94.37	Oregon	80.43	Mississippi	59.70	New Jersey	60.30	New Jersey	4.64
Virginia	93.90	Maine	80.13	Nevada	59.26	Oklahoma	59.91	Oklahoma	4.58
Kansas	93.46	Alaska	79.72	Kentucky	59.07	South Carolina	59.74	South Carolina	4.56
Missouri	93.46	Indiana	78.51	Massachusetts	58.88	Colorado	59.72	Colorado	4.49
Oregon	93.33	Illinois	78.14	Connecticut	58.62	Alabama	59.16	Alabama	4.46
Idaho	92.67	California	77.28	New York	58.56	New Hampshire	58.81	New Hampshire	4.31
Guam	92.65	Kentucky	77.27	Oregon	58.33	Arkansas	58.67	Arkansas	4.28
South Carolina	92.50	Connecticut	77.08	Missouri	58.16	Maryland	58.62	Maryland	4.13
Rhode Island	92.35	Missouri	76.54	Louisiana	56.80	Rhode Island	58.39	Rhode Island	4.10
Maryland	91.88	Puerto Rico	75.75	Maine	56.62	Alaska	57.85	Alaska	4.00
Michigan	91.52	Louisiana	75.67	Tennessee	56.22	Nevada	57.53	Nevada	3.98
Nebraska	91.39	Virgin Islands	75.48	Delaware	56.08	Maine	57.42	Maine	3.84
Massachusetts	91.10	Kansas	74.98	Idaho	55.37	Connecticut	57.20	Connecticut	3.65
Tennessee	90.93	New Mexico	73.70	Michigan	55.03	Minnesota	57.20	Minnesota	3.60
New York	90.55	Oklahoma	71.30	Rhode Island	54.90	Kansas	56.50	Kansas	3.45
Louisiana	90.50	Mississippi	70.66	Alabama	54.45	Vermont	56.09	Vermont	3.29

Child Support Enforcement Program Incentive Payments: Background and Policy Issues

State	Paternity Establish-ment Percentage	State	Cases with Orders Percentage	State	Current Collections Percentage	State	Arrearage Cases Percentage	State	Cost Effective-ness Score
Ohio	90.44	Tennessee	68.20	Arizona	53.14	Arizona	54.69	New Mexico	2.71
Mississippi	90.16	Florida	67.95	South Carolina	53.06	South Carolina	53.85	Guam	2.31
Dist. of Columbia	90.00	South Carolina	67.81	Virgin Islands	52.26	Virgin Islands	52.32	California	2.29
Virgin Islands	89.75	Arizona	66.41	Dist. of Columbia	51.45	Dist. of Columbia	51.89	Delaware	2.23
Illinois	84.95	Nevada	65.81	Puerto Rico	51.11	Puerto Rico	50.43	Dist. of Columbia	2.13
Delaware	77.98	Alabama	58.54	Hawaii	50.97	Hawaii	45.37	Virgin Islands	$1.98

Source: Table prepared by the Congressional Research Service based on data from the Office of Child Support Enforcement, Department of Health and Human Services.

Note: The paternity establishment percentage can be greater than 100% because states can take credit for paternities established for children of any age and compare that number established to the number of births outside of marriage for a single year.

Author Contact Information

Carmen Solomon-Fears
Specialist in Social Policy
csolomonfears@crs.loc.gov, 7-7306

www.ingramcontent.com/pod-product-compliance
Lightning Source LLC
Chambersburg PA
CBHW081616170526
45166CB00009B/2996